# SELLING YOURSELF INTO A JOB

## A Systematic Guide to Finding Your Dream Job

William Swansen

William Swansen
Visit my website at www.sellingyourselfintoajob.com

Printed in the United States of America

First Printing: November 2017
Create Space

ISBN-13: 978-1979934565

*This book is dedicated to my Daughter Danielle.
Dani, you are my Muse, my Collaborator, and, most
importantly my Friend. Without you, this project would not
have been possible. Thank You. Dad*

# CONTENTS

# Forward

I

t was the fall of 2009 and my daughter had graduated from one of the most prestigious universities in the US the previous spring. She had spent the summer looking for a job but had become frustrated due to her lack of success in the pursuit of her first career position. It didn't help that she had graduated school at the depth of a recession. Even seasoned professionals with years of experience were having trouble finding a job after going through a company layoff. After numerous email exchanges and some long phone conversations, it dawned on me that maybe there was something I could do to help her.

I had spent my career of three decades as a professional salesperson in the information technology industry. Over the years I crafted my skills at convincing people to purchase the products and services of the companies that I represented. I used standard sales techniques that were time-tested and common across industries and geographies.

I realized that finding a job was nothing more than another sales campaign. My daughter was trying to sell her services to a prospective employer in return for reasonable compensation. I thought that if we could apply the skills and techniques used by salespeople to her job search efforts, she would be more successful. When I discussed this with her she had run out of ideas and so readily agreed to give it a try.

Together we embarked on a sales campaign to market my daughter's services. First, I created a set of collateral materials (brochures) for her including an updated resume, a portfolio of cover letter (email) templates and a personal website in the form of a LinkedIn profile.

We then identified potential employers (customers) in her area and determined who the prospective hiring managers (decision makers) were. She sent emails containing her resume and using the cover letter templates to these contacts (prospects) and followed up with additional emails and phone calls.

Within several weeks she had multiple invitations for interviews. I helped her prepare for the interviews (product demonstrations) much like a salesperson prepares for a sales presentation. I coached her on how to conduct herself during the interview and how to follow up afterward.

45 days after beginning this campaign, she had three job offers related to her field of study and her degree. I helped her negotiate (close) these and she selected the one best suited for her talents and which provided the best combination of compensation and benefits.

I then coached her on what to do during her first 90 days of employment to ensure that she would succeed in this position and to prepare her or advancement to the next one (customer experience.)

Soon, word got out about our success and other family members and friends began contacting me asking if I could help them in their job search and career development. As I helped more people, I became better educated about the job search process. Although I was still working full-time as a salesperson, the process people used to find jobs and advance their careers was fascinating to me. I began to follow bloggers who wrote about this topic and read everything I could find on the Internet. I also volunteered my services to help disadvantaged youth and homeless families get back into the workforce. After 10 years of doing this on a volunteer basis, I decided I would like to do it full-time. I quit my job, left the information technology industry, and started a business as the Job Search Strategist and Career Coach. It was very scary at the time, but I knew based on all I had learned that it was the right thing to do. I knew I would be successful at this because of my passion for both the profession and for helping people.

This book is another step in my quest to assist people with their career advancement. In it, I have summarized everything I have learned about the job search process over the last 10 years. I go into more detail about the system I developed to organize the job search process and make it more effective and efficient. I break down each component of the system and provide instructions on how to create job search collateral materials and identify potential employers and hiring managers. You'll learn how to conduct a sales campaign, informing employers about your availability to provide your services to them. I then discuss the interview process and the three stages of a successful interview, which include research, what to do during the interview, and what to do afterward. Next, I provide coaching on how to negotiate a successful job offer and what to do during your first 90 days on the job to ensure your success. The book concludes with a description of how to run the job search process including scheduling, tasks, tracking your activity and other components of the job search system I developed. I explore each topic in depth and provide links where you can obtain additional job search resources.

My goal in writing this book is to make the job search process easier to understand. I provide a system which people can execute regardless of what profession or industry they work in. Since searching for a job is one most stressful activities people encounter during their career, I also try to make the process as easy and enjoyable as possible. As you will see in the book, one of the key themes is repetition. The more times you do something, the better you get at it. The better you are at a task, the more you enjoy doing it.

I hope that after reading this book and using the resources detailed inside of it, you will be able to execute your own job search and develop a clear plan for your career advancement. Even though I work as a Job Search Strategist and Career Coach, my goal is to put myself out of business by enabling people to do this themselves. However, if after reading this book you still have questions, need additional resources, or would like to enlist me to help you with your job search, please feel free to reach out to me. I will help you in any way that I can.


Sincerely,

William Swansen
bill@sellingyourselfintoajob.com
www.sellingyourselfintoajob.com

# Introduction – Finding a Job is a Job

---

*"The greatest thing in this world is not so much where we stand, as in what direction we are moving." —Oliver Wendell Holmes*

---

G et ready for the hardest job that you will ever have. Whether you are currently employed and looking for something better, or out of work and need to get back into the workforce, you are about to embark on one of the most difficult jobs you will have during your career. That is the job of finding a job.

There are two main reasons that finding a job is so difficult. First, few people have been formally trained in the process of getting a job. Second, there are so many ways to pursue this that it is difficult to know how to get started and what to do. Fortunately, there are thousands of resources available to assist you with your job search efforts. These include job boards, blogs, resume writing services, career coaches, and a myriad of others. The problem then becomes which ones of these do you use and how much, if anything should you pay for them. That is what this guide is all about. I have spent years reviewing the techniques and tools used by job search professionals and career coaches and have synthesized this information into an easy to follow step-by-step guide. This book will help you understand the various components of a successful job search process. It will also help you to execute your job search in an organized and systematic way. As a result, you will spend less time and get better results while searching for your next ideal job. Thousands of people have used this approach and have been successful in their job search process.

It is important that you approach the job search process in an organized manner. Most people fail when searching for a job because they are not consistent in what they do and how often they do it. Also, they do not take advantage of the opportunity to reuse processes and materials they have already created. In just about any endeavor in life, practice makes perfect. The more times you repeat a task the easier it gets and the better you are at it. This applies to the job search process as well. As you will see in later chapters in this book, repetition, and consistency are critical in finding a job quickly and with the least amount of the effort possible.

Another key component of a successful job search process is treating it like a job. This means getting up each day with a full schedule of activities, and putting in as much time as you would if you were working at an actual job. However, you do not need to devote all your time looking for a job. I recommend dividing your time between three areas:

1. Looking for a job

2. Working part-time

3. Volunteering

While the first of these is obvious, the other two may have you scratching your head a bit. You may be asking yourself, "Why should I work part-time and spend time volunteering if I what I really need is a full-time job?" The answer is simple. Working part-time in any job you can find will not only provide you with some income needed to pay your immediate expenses but will also keep you active and in the workforce. This keeps your work and interpersonal skills sharp and fresh. On the other hand, volunteering will expose you to opportunities which could become permanent employment. Helping others who may be less fortunate than you will also make you feel good about yourself and help you to maintain your self-esteem during the job search process. I discuss this in more detail in the in the section which describes the job search system.

I have organized this book into several sections, each of which addresses a specific component of the job search process. You do not need to read these in sequential order. You can go directly to the part of the job search which you are either currently engaged in or need some help with. Throughout the book, there are links to resources which may be helpful in your job search process.

# Personal Profile and Career Assessment

---

*"If you don't know where you are going, you'll end up someplace else" –*
*Yogi Bera*

---

Y ogi Berra is known for his oddball, but sometimes insightful quotes. This one is a perfect description of the first mistake most job seekers make during their effort to get a new position or advance their career. It is a "ready, fire, aim" exercise where they start off pursuing opportunities before considering what they would really enjoy and be good at. Confucius once said, "If you do what you love, you will never work a day in your life." Most of us must spend an average of 8 hours a day, 5 days a week, 12 months a year for about 50 years working to earn a living. That is 100,000 hours or about 14% of our life. You can spend this time enjoying what you are doing, or you can spend it looking at the clock wishing you were someplace (anyplace!) else. Additionally, people who do what they truly love tend to be good at it and therefore are successful in their careers.

## My Story

My personal story about how I found my ultimate profession illustrates how both the right and the wrong career choices can impact your life.

My first job was delivering papers when I was only 13 years old. I worked consistently after that at a variety of positions. These included bagging groceries, mowing lawns, doing odd jobs and pumping gas. These experiences both instilled in me a strong work ethic and a clear picture of what I did not do for a long-term career.

I excelled in high school so by the time I reached my senior year I was only attending classes during the morning. This gave me the remainder of the day and most of my evenings free from homework to do something else. One of the things I chose to do was to take some college-level courses to get a head start on my college career. Since I had done well on my advanced placement tests, doing this would enable me to start college already having completed my freshman year and my core courses.

One of the classes I took was in the field of sociology. I had always found this subject fascinating and thought that perhaps I would pursue a career as a sociologist or social worker. Like any impressionable teenager, I immediately became enamored with the social work profession. I convinced myself that this should be my lifelong career.

Upon entering college, I continued to take courses in sociology and declared this as my major. I enjoyed my studies and the theoretical knowledge I was acquiring. This was the type of work I was born to do.

During the summer between my sophomore and junior year in college, I signed up for an internship working with a local social services agency. I looked forward to putting my theoretical knowledge to use and helping the less fortunate people in my community. My first assignment was with an organization that worked with welfare recipients to help find them jobs. At first, I loved the work and felt proud of the contribution I was making. But soon I became bogged down in the paperwork required by the agency and the bureaucracy that was inherent with most government related organizations. It did not take long before I was spending most of my time dealing with the administrative tasks required by the job. I found that my time wasn't spent interfacing with the clients and helping them to realize their goal of getting off welfare and becoming self-supporting.

Upon completing my internship, it became apparent to me that this was not the type of work that I would enjoy doing as a career. While I was passionate about the work and enjoyed the idea of helping others, I did not like the bureaucratic and administrative side of the profession.

Since I was not sure what to do, I left school and took a full-time job at an auto dealership. I knew this was not what I wanted to do as a career, but with a little direction, it provided me some income and time to figure out what to do next. Unfortunately, the next step toward my ultimate career was worse than the first one I had taken.

Having had time to consider my situation, I decided that I would return to school and pursue a degree in the field of chemistry. I had always done well in this subject during high school and enjoyed the related courses such as math and physics. I changed schools, transferred as many credits as I could, and began my academic pursuit toward a degree in chemistry. At first, things went well, and I enjoyed the classes I was taking. I convinced myself that I had made the right decision and was on the path towards my ultimate career. I even got a job working in a chemical plant as a lab technician. I enjoyed this work which confirmed that I had made the right choice. However, two things occurred which would change my mind and put me on the path to my eventual permanent career.

First, I began to perform poorly in several of my classes. I did not have as strong of a foundation in math and some of the other related courses as I thought I did and quickly fell behind in the college-level classes. Since I was not doing well I no longer enjoyed the coursework and I became concerned about my ability to finish the program.

The second thing was that my company asked me to accompany a sales team into the field to support a demonstration of one of our products. The trip exposed me to the sales and marketing process for the products our company produced. I liked the way the salespeople interacted with their customers and how they used their interpersonal skills to create a relationship with them. I saw immediately that the selling process was simply satisfying a need a customer had with the products the company produced. It occurred to me that this was very close to what I had started out doing during my career as a sociologist; Directing my clients toward the resources they needed to reach their life goals.

After several more sales trips, I became convinced that this is what I wanted to do for a living. However, my "sunk cost" was the only thing that concerned me. This was the time I had already invested towards obtaining a degree as a chemist. I met with the school's counseling office and learned about a new program which allowed students to design their own majors. I put together a program that combined science classes and business courses, which was ideal for someone who was involved in marketing a complex product to customers. Both the school and the company I worked for agreed to my new major and within 18 months I graduated with a degree in Technical Sales.

The company I was working for transferred me to the sales organization and I began putting my new skills to use. I was never happier. In addition to enjoying my new career, I found out I was good at it and was succeeding at closing business for my company. I knew that I had done the right thing and proceeded on a career path which would eventually run for almost 40 years.

Finding a profession which you love and enjoy doing takes time. It is a result of discovering your natural talents, determining what interests you, and finding out if you would enjoy doing it for a living. The process involves both formal and informal training, trial and error, observing other people working in your dream profession, and an honest self-assessment. There is also an element of "luck" and circumstance involved. Often our career finds us through actions and events beyond our control. Once you have an idea of what you are passionate about, determine what type of jobs will allow you to do it while earning a living.

# Personal Assessment

The first step in the career assessment process is to determine your personality type and what your strengths and weaknesses are. We are all different and excel at different activities. Characteristics of leadership, compassion, empathy, decisiveness, attention to detail, the ability to see the big picture and many more traits set us all apart from each other.

There are multiple resources available on the Internet to help you determine some of your work-related personality traits. However, the one I prefer is easy to access and provides instant feedback. It is available at https://bornforthisbook.com/. Chris Guillebeau, author of "Born for This" and other career-related publications provides a 14-question quiz to help you categorize some of your major personality traits. You can then use these to determine the type of jobs that you would excel at and enjoy doing.

## Joy, Flow, Money

Guillebeau succinctly summarizes the three characteristics that will help you determined the type of work you should do. These are:

1. Joy
2. Flow
3. Money

The concept is simple. If you enjoy what you are doing (Joy), find it easy to accomplish (Flow), and you can generate an income by doing it (Money) then this is very likely the profession that you should choose. These characteristics combined will result in success where you make money, advance your career, and get up each day looking forward to going to work.

Whether you use the "Joy, Flow, Money" methodology or some other system, before you start on the process of choosing a career and finding your next job, you need to figure out what you would like to do and where you are going. Once you have a goal, you can then create a plan for how to get there.

## Ikigai

Another method you can use to discover your career path is "Ikigai." This is the Japanese concept in which the four critical criteria for life intersect and result in a definition of "A Reason to Live." The method begins with asking yourself four fundamental questions:

1. What do you love?
2. What are you good at?
3. What does the world need from you?
4. What can you get paid for?

Once you list everything you can think of for each of these questions, review your answers and highlight the common ones. These will describe the type of work you should be doing. You then only need apply these to your professional aspirations, an industry and a place you want to live and work in.

# Career Plan

After you have completed your assessment and discovered what you are good at, what you enjoy and what the world is willing to pay you to do, you can begin to work on your plan for your career. This will help you determine what steps are necessary to get you to both your next job and ultimately to your ideal career goal.

An easy way to develop a career plan is to start at the end. Determine what you would like to be doing at the end of your career. Your goal should include a profession, industry, job, and target income. Then, work backward to identify each position that precedes your ultimate job. As an example, being a President of a large company is usually preceded by being a Vice President, which comes after you are a Director, and so on. Each position should include a title, brief description, estimated income, and target date to attain it. Eventually, you will be at the point in your planning process where you will be describing your next job, which is the one that will start you on the path toward your ultimate position.

When describing your next job, you will need to provide more details. These will include:

• The Job Title

- Description of the Duties
- Requirements needed to obtain the position, including:
  - Education
  - Experience
  - Skill Set
- Target Industry
- Geography
- Income you can anticipate

Knowing these characteristics of your job, you can now begin to create your job search strategy and move to the first step in the process; Creating your job search collateral materials. These include your resume, cover letters (i.e., email templates) and online career profile (LinkedIn).

# Your Resume

T his quote about resumes sums up how most people approach the task of constructing a document to sell themselves to prospective employers. Most Human Resource (HR) professionals and hiring managers have learned to look past the exaggerations, accolades, and clichés many people include in their resume. Their job is to determine if the job candidate has the appropriate training, experience, and skills to do the job they are looking to fill.

Your resume is how you present yourself to your "customers", which are prospective employers. It is the second chance you will have to make a good first impression (the first being your cover letter/email.) The purpose of the resume is to get you to the next step in the process, which is the interview. You will not get a job based on just your resume, no matter how good it is. However, you will not get a chance to interview for a job unless your resume is written correctly.

Most people approach a resume as a historical record of their work experience. It is actually a preview of how you can help prospective employers achieve their organizational objectives. This is how an interviewer approaches your resume. They have a requirement and are looking for a qualified individual who can help them fulfill this. Your resume needs to convey your qualifications for the position and how you can assist them to meet their requirements. You do this by demonstrating your skills, experience, and talents relevant to the job they need you to do. The history of your work experience provides evidence for how you acquired the skills and talents you can apply to help the prospective employer. It shows how you can achieve their objectives and why you qualify for the job they are trying to fill. The key is to focus on them and their requirements and not on you and your history. Many people do the later and fall in love with their resume, thinking that prospective employers will love it as well. Try not to fall into this trap.

An easy way verify that your resume addresses the needs of the employer is to ask the following question:

"Is the information in my resume telling the employer how I can –

- Help them Make Money?
- Help them Save Money?
- Help them Save Time?

If not, why should they hire me?"

The bottom line is to focus on achieving an objective for any organization you may want to work for. To do this you need to utilize as few resources as are necessary, and at the least cost possible and as quickly as possible. Any investment they make in any type of resource, human or another kind, needs to help advance them toward the achievement of their objective. Anything else is wasteful or a distraction. You can apply this rule to any type of organization whether they are a business, non-profit, governmental agency or a community service. (NOTE: You can also apply this same principle to your own job search.)

Now that you know the purpose of a resume and the information it should provide to a prospective employer, you can begin to focus on the structure and content of the resume.

The structure of the resume should enable you to convey the information you want the employer to know as quickly and clearly as possible. Studies indicate that an employer only spends 10-15 seconds reviewing a resume. In this short amount of time, they decide whether they would like to learn more about you. The Society of Human Resource Professionals (SHRP) goes even further and says hiring managers form an opinion about you in about six seconds. In either case, you need to tell your story quickly and clearly.

A good rule of thumb to use is to assume that the employer will only view the first half of the first page of your resume before they form an impression of you. They then decide if they want to read the balance of the resume to learn more about you. An easy way to see what the employer will see is to fold the first page of your resume in half widthwise and review the information. Does it provide the employer with a quick and clear summary of your qualifications for the job? If not, you have some editing to do.

# Resume Layout

The first thing to know about creating a resume is that there is no "perfect" or "ideal" resume. Since each person reviewing a resume is an individual with their own tastes and preferences, each will approach a resume from their own perspective. It would be impossible to create a resume that would appeal to everyone. What you should aim for is to have a well-structured, succinct and organized resume. It should clearly present your talents, skills, experience, and personality to a prospective employer.

## Number of Pages

The biggest myth or misconception about a resume is the ideal number of pages. Many people feel that there is a one-page limit to a resume. Or they feel that more than two or three pages are too much. Both assumptions are incorrect. The right answer is that a resume should be as long as it needs to be to convey your qualifications to a prospective employer. If you have limited work experience one page is adequate. If you are a seasoned professional and have worked on many projects relevant to the job you are applying for, then you may have a resume with as many as four to five pages.

The important factors when deciding if your resume is the correct length are:

- Is all the content relevant?
- Are you being concise and to the point and not embellishing the content in order to impress the reader with your use of language?
- Have you put the most important content in the first half of the first page in order to capture the reader's attention and entice them to read the balance of the resume?
- Does each item in the resume demonstrate your qualifications for the position?
- Is any of the information about your work experience or other qualifications repeated?

By following these guidelines, you will end up with a resume that is the appropriate length, conveys your qualifications for the position, and will keep the reader's attention from the beginning to the end.

### Font & Graphics

The font you choose and any graphic elements are not that critical. I recommend either a sans-serif font (Calibri or Arial) or Times Roman. These are clear and format well across a variety of document editors and readers. Keep graphic elements to a minimum. Employers are more interested in content than appearance and are not likely to select your resume over others because of how it looks. Use any graphic elements only to help organize the information, delineate one section of the resume from another, or to draw attention to an important item in the resume.

### Colors & Pictures

Never use colors or pictures unless you are applying for a position that involves some design or artistic creation. Again, these will only serve to distract the reader from the content of the resume. It could be a negative element if the employer does not like the color or image.

### Columns

A final consideration for the general layout and format of the resume is the number of columns you use. I recommend a single column, with no sidebars. People will typically use sidebars, or areas adjacent to the main body of their resume to provide a summary of their skills, for their contact information, or to put other content which they would like to highlight. The problem with this is that most people read in a traditional left to right, top to bottom flow. If you have multiple columns or areas in your resume, you force the reader to jump around to find the information they are most interested in. While it may make sense to you (mainly because you spent hours designing it,) it will be foreign to the employer. Keep the layout simple and easy to follow and your resume will be more effective in getting you to the next step in the process, which is the interview.

# Resume Format

The following is a recommended format for a resume that will accomplish this objective.

### Header

The Header section of the resume contains your contact information. I recommend you put this in a header so that it will be visible on each page of the resume. This ensures that the employer is aware of whose resume they are reviewing. This sounds obvious, but in the competitive job environment, employers may receive hundreds of resumes for each position they are looking to fill and may review dozens. It is not uncommon for them to like a candidate, but then for them to mistakenly contact someone else for the interview.

The Header should contain the following information:

- Name (First and Last; a Middle Initial is OK – 14 Point Type (no larger)
- Phone Number (Mobile is best, and the same size as the font in the body of the resume)
- eMail (your personal email, with your first and last name if possible; nothing fancy or "cute")
- LinkedIn Profile URL

The layout of the header can vary if it is clear and takes up as little space as possible. Since the type in the header will "fade", it will work best if the header is in bold type.

Here is a sample layout that works for most resumes:

**Jane Smith**

**555-123-4567**
**Jane.smith@gmail.com**
**LinkedIn https://www.linkedin.com/in/jane-smith**

## Job Title and Summary

The best way to get an employer to start visualizing you as qualified for the position they are looking to fill is to add a "Job Title" to the beginning of your resume. The Job Title should align with the job position you are applying for and reflect what you have done in the past. It can be somewhat general, and contain terms like "Professional" or "Specialist." An example of this would be if the Job Posting was for a Human Resources Manager, your title in your resume could be "HR Professional", "Human Resources Specialist" or "Manager of Personnel."

The Summary section should follow the Job Title. There is no need to provide a heading for this because it is a description of the job title you have already used. Additionally, it is evident that this is a summary so there is no reason to title it as such.

The summary should be in the first person and should highlight the main skills, talents, and experience you have. Again, it needs to demonstrate your qualifications for the position and convey how you will help the employer, "make money, save money or save time." An easy way to write this is to review the requirements listed in the job posting. Use the same terminology and phrases in the posting to describe your skills and experience. This will align you with the job posting and enable the employer to begin to visualize you in the position.

Here is an example of a Job Title and Summary statement:

**Human Resources Professional**

> I am an experienced Human Resources Professional, adept at selecting talent which meets the requirements of an organization's staffing needs in an efficient and effective manner. I have developed a screening system which resulted in shortening the time required to fill vacant positions and reducing new hire turnover by 20%. I am skilled at writing job descriptions and posting them to the appropriate social media and online job boards. I have trained hiring managers to conduct professional interviews and am comfortable assessing candidates' qualifications and making hiring recommendations to management. I am bilingual and fluent in English and Spanish, both written and verbal.

The descriptions in this summary match the job posting and convey how the applicant can perform the job duties required for the position. It also highlights an accomplishment at a former position which saved the previous employer both time and money. The summary should be succinct and should motivate the prospective employer to read the balance of the resume. They can then validate the claims made in the summary. They will also discover the details of how the applicant accomplished what they have described.

## Skills

A summarized listing of skills is an optional section of the resume. Whether you include this will depend on the nature of the job you are applying for, the description of your skills in the summary section, and how important specific skills are to the job. Many jobs are general in nature and your summary and subsequent employment experience section will aptly describe your skills. Other jobs may be unique enough or require very specific skills, so a listing of your skills may be appropriate.

There are some general guidelines if you elect to have a Skills section in your resume. These will make the section more effective and ensure that it will enhance your resume rather than distract from it.

The number of skills should be more than four and less than eight in most cases. Fewer would not justify a separate section for these and you can include the skills in the summary section. More will dilute the effectiveness of this section and likely result in the reader becoming less interested in learning more about you. If you have multiple skills and all of them are applicable to the job you are applying for, they should be part of your employment experience.

The format of the skills section depends on the description of each skill. If they are all short and contain only one to three words, then bullets in multiple columns work best. This will preserve the valuable "first half of the first page" real estate of your resume and allow the employer to quickly read all the skills. An example of this type of formatting is:

## Skills

- Writing Job Descriptions
- Training Management in Interview Skills
- Screening Candidates
- Employee Onboarding
- Posting to Job Boards
- Employee Benefit Programs
- Working with Recruiters
- Records Management

If the descriptions of the skills are longer and more elaborate, then you should still use a bulleted format, but only a single column. This will make them easier to read and will match the format of the rest of the resume.

Here is an example of this format:

### Skills

- Writing effective job descriptions resulting in better pools of candidates
- Skilled at screening applicants and presenting only qualified candidates to hiring managers
- Experienced working with recruiters, headhunters and other employment personnel
- Able to quickly onboard new hires and make them productive in the shortest time possible
- Familiar with employee benefit programs; able to select the appropriate program for an organization and manage it efficiently

## Employment Experience

There are two approaches to writing the Employment Experience; Chronological or Functional. Both can be effective if used for the appropriate job or profession. In general, a chronological listing of a person's employment experience is the most used format and is appropriate for most positions.

**Chronological Resume**

A chronological resume provides the prospective employer with a history of your work experience. This way they can learn about the experience you have had and the progression of your career. The order of the jobs should begin with your most recent job first, then list your previous jobs in reverse order. There is no real limit on the number of jobs you can list. The general rule is no more than 20 years' worth of experience unless adding more enhances your qualifications for the job you are applying for or your early positions were long-term and extend the resume past the 20-year rule. The rationale behind this is that with today's advancements in technology, job requirements and duties change faster than they used to. Therefore, older experience may no longer be relevant to the current requirements for the position.

The job listings in a chronological resume should start with the Title of the position. Most Titles are descriptive enough and may not require any additional embellishment. If not, then a brief description of the job should follow the title.

The next part of the job listing is the Company, Location, and the Dates Employed. Again, if the company is not well known or you are applying for a position outside of the industry or different from the occupation of your previous employer, then a brief description of what the company did is appropriate. The part of the job description provides the prospective employer with an idea of what type of organizational experience you have and whether it matches their requirements.

The final section of the header for each job description is a summary of the responsibilities and duties of the position. This should enable the prospective employer to understand what you did for your previous employer. If possible, it should match some of the responsibilities of the job you are applying for. There is no need to be too detailed in this description or to list any significant accomplishment you achieved in this position. Describe these in the body of the job listing.

Format this part of the Employment Experience section like this example;

**Human Resources Manager**
**General Motors    Detroit, MI**                                    2010 – 2017

Managed a department of 12 human resources professionals responsible for staffing and managing the employment-related details of the assembly line staff at the Light Truck Division of a major automotive company. Reported to the Vice President of Finance and was responsible for the day to day human resources activities for over 2000 employees.

The next section of each of your job descriptions is the listing of your accomplishments, achievements, responsibilities, and duties. These are listed in this order on purpose because this is their relative importance. The duties of most jobs are evident and job postings will list these for any position that interests you. What an employer will be looking for is what you can do for them to help them achieve their objectives. They will assume you can perform the duties of the job. Therefore, you should demonstrate what you achieved for your last employers as evidence of what you can do for the prospective employer.

Another key element of demonstrating your achievements and accomplishments in your previous positions is to use specific and detailed numbers. Dollar amounts, percentages, the amount of time by which you reduced a process or task are all important and will impress the hiring manager. Vague and general statements will not.

Limit the listing of what you did in your previous positions to no more than 5 or 6 items. If properly written, these will provide plenty of evidence of your ability to do the job you are applying for. Any more may cause the reader to lose interest or even doubt your sincerity. You will have the opportunity to discuss all your accomplishments during the interview, so you do not need to list them on the resume. Also, don't repeat accomplishments you had in previous positions. Each position should be unique and should demonstrate a continuum of job skill development, increased responsibility, and the scope of contributions you have made to the employer. Finally, list the accomplishments in a bulleted format to make them easy to read.

Here are some samples of accomplishments for a position as a Human Resources Manager.

- Reduced the time to onboard a new employee by 25%, thereby increasing their productivity and contribution to the company's objectives.
- Decreased the department's budget by 10%, saving the organization $100K per year by implementing automated Applicant Tracking Systems (ATS) and eliminating postings on fee-based job boards.
- Increased employee retention by 10% using early intervention techniques in response to disgruntled employee complaints.
- Attained consistent "Superior" ratings during annual reviews by department supervisors.
- Noted as "Employee of the Year" during my last two years with the company.

Note the "Did/By" format of these statements. Each one described what the applicant "Did" and then told the reader how they accomplished it, or "By." This style will help the hiring manager envision how you can help them solve their problems or accomplish their objectives which may be the same as your previous employers. It also provides proof of the accomplishments you are claiming by describing how you did them.

**Functional Resume**

The Functional Resume is like the Chronological Resume in everything except for the Employment Experience. Rather than listing each job in reverse chronological order, the Functional Resume lists your skills, talents, duties, and experiences in separate, related groups. You can reference the jobs at which you did these within the functional section of the resume if it is appropriate or helps to enhance the hiring manager's understanding of your experience. The main part of this section describes the function you performed and the components of the function.

A Functional Resume isn't used as much as a Chronological Resume. However, it may be more appropriate for certain positions where what you can do is more important than what you have done and where you did it. Examples include medical professions, educators, government employees, and creative jobs such as writers, artists, and performers. People may be more apt to use a Functional Resume if they are transitioning to a new career or have gaps in their employment history.

When writing a Functional Resume, it is easiest to organize your experience around a theme or group of related functions. You then list bulleted descriptions of the job activities related to the functions, highlighting the accomplishments related to the group. Prioritize groups of functions by the most important or relevant to the job position you are applying for.

An example of the Functional Description looks like this:

### Skills & Experience
**Recruitment**
- Write compelling job descriptions which attract qualified candidates.
- Familiar with major Job Boards and other online recruitment resources.
- Experienced with conducting on-campus recruitment events.

**Interviewing**
- Capable of conducting a variety of different types of interviews including functional, informational and behavioral.

- Skilled at screening candidates and making recommendations to department hiring managers.

**Employee Onboarding**
- Experience in creating and implementing employee onboarding processes and procedures.
- Employee Benefits Specialist with knowledge of competitive benefit programs and providers.
- Skilled at employee orientation and mentoring.

The next section of the functional resume is "Achievements." This describes significant achievements in previous jobs you have held. List the achievements without reference to the specific employer or time frame. Do so unless this information isn't required to describe the achievement or add credibility to it.

An example of the Achievement section of the Functional Resume is:

## Significant Achievements
- Reduced employee onboarding time be 25% while increasing new employee retention after one year by 10%.

- Renegotiated the Employee Benefits Program for a staff of over 1000 at Acme Manufacturing, saving the company over $1M per year and providing the employees with a more robust healthcare package.

- Recruited the CEO and President for ABC Corporation, meeting the Board of Director's criteria and time frame. These executives subsequently led the company to record revenues and profits during their first two years with the organization.

The balance of a Functional Resume is the same as the Chronological Resume except for the Employment Experience section. The previous jobs are still listed in chronological order. They may have a brief description of the organization and/or the position, but don't include any details. Here is an example of this:

## Employment Experience

**Human Resources Manager**
**General Motors    Detroit, MI**                                2010 - 2017
Managed a department of 12 human resources professionals responsible for staffing and managing the employment-related details of the assembly line staff at the Light Truck Division of a major automotive company. Reported to the Vice President of Finance and was responsible for the day-to-day human resources activities for over 2000 employees.

**Human Resources Specialist**

**Acme Manufacturing**　　　**Detroit, MI**　　　　　　　　2007 – 2009

Responsible for employee onboarding and benefits administration for a manufacturing company with over 1000 employees.

**Recruitment Manager**

**ABC Corporation**　　　　**Chicago, IL**　　　　　　　　2003 – 2007

Recruited key executives and senior managers for a Financial Services provider focused on business lending.

# Education

The next section for both types of resumes is the Education history. This provides details about any formal and informal education and training you have received. Much like the Employment Experience, list Education history in reverse chronological order, with the highest degree or education achievement listed first. Each formal educational experience or degree should contain; the Institution, Location, Date of Graduation (Month and Year,) Degree earned, Concentration, and if applicable, and any Honors received. Additional training or certifications should contain the Title of the Training or Certification, the Date Acquired and the Name of the Certificate (if applicable.)

If the highest degree is in college, do not include high school degrees. Also, do not include in-house training or continuing education credits either offered by an employer or required by a professional license. Also, do not include any industry-sponsored workshops or seminars unless they resulted in specific certification or additional credentials related to the job title.

The Education section of the Resume would look like the following:

**Education**

**University of Michigan**　　Ann Arbor, MI　　　　　　June 2003

**Masters of Business Administration, Human Resources**

Graduated Magna Cum Laude

**Michigan State University**　East Lansing, MI　　　　　May 2001

**Bachelor's Degree, Business Administration**

**Society of Human Resources Professionals (SHRP)**

HR Professional Certification　　　　　　　　　　　October 2011

## Optional Sections

Depending on your specific profession and work history, you may want to include some other optional sections in your resume. These are intended to provide the hiring manager with additional information about your qualifications or experience which are relevant to the position but aren't detailed in the other sections of the resume. Place these sections after the Education section of the resume.

Several possible Optional Sections of your resume are:

· **Volunteer Experience** – Any work you have done for volunteer organizations, especially if it is a related experience to the occupation or position that interests you.

· **Awards and Recognition** – This would include any recognition and award received for either professional or personal achievements. List scholarly recognition in the Education section of the resume.

· **Board Membership** – Being a member of a Board of Directors for an organization demonstrates your expertise and recognition of your skills by other members of your profession.

· **Membership in Industry Groups or Professional Associations** – These can include trade groups, professional associations related to credentials required by the profession, or honorific societies.

· **Publications** – These may be professional papers, books, articles or formal research papers.

· **Projects** – Several professions involve working on specific projects and listing these may demonstrate your qualifications to do similar work for the prospective employer

## Personal Information

Including Personal Information in your resume is optional. Base the choice to do this on your individual situation, the position you are applying for, and how much you know about the hiring manager or the employer.

The argument for including personal information is that it provides the reader with some insight into you as an individual. One factor every employer uses to determine if they should interview you in addition to your qualifications and what you can contribute to the organization's mission or business objectives is how well you will fit into their corporate culture. Employers want to hire individuals who will get along with their current staff and even add some "personality" to the organization. Adding personal information to your resume will enable them to determine this and may make you stand out from other job applicants.

Another reason to include personal information in a resume is that it may enable the hiring manager to connect with you due to a common experience or interest. If you have traveled to an interesting location or enjoy a hobby or sporting activity shared by the reader, it may be the extra incentive they need to invite you to an interview. It will also create a connection between you and the interviewer that can "break the ice" at the start of the interview.

When including Personal Information in a resume, you should follow these guidelines:

- Keep it brief and use a bulleted list.

- Avoid any controversial items (religion, politics, activities that are not mainstream or considered "socially acceptable," etc.)

- Don't embellish and be honest; they will most likely ask you about some of your personal interests during the interview and you want to be able to discuss them honestly and based on your experience.

- Avoid personal information related to your age, race, family status or anything else that may subject the employer to a claim of discrimination in hiring.

Here is an example of what a Personal Information section of a resume would look like:

### Personal Information

- Travel Enthusiast, having visited six of the seven continents in the world.

- Avid water sports participant who enjoys surfing, sailing, diving and water skiing.

- Golfer and volunteer for several annual PGA events.

- Volunteer for Habitat for Humanity. Participated in six projects to date.

## Conclusion

There is no such thing as a "Perfect" resume. Everyone is an individual with a unique personality, set of experiences and portfolio of talents and skills. The person reviewing your resume is also unique, with their own perspective on hiring, set of preferences and a history of experiences. There is no guarantee that every hiring manager will be impressed with your resume no matter how well it is written.

The best you can do is to organize your resume in clear and concise fashion, include keywords and phrases related to the jobs you are interested in and describe your skills and qualifications based on your professional experience and education. This will help you communicate to the employer that you are the right person for the job (at least in your opinion!) Doing this should eventually lead to invitations to interview and ultimately job offers.

The next task is to get the employer to review your resume. This is the objective of your cover letter, which is discussed in the next chapter.

# Sample Resume

## John Smith

● Vista, CA 92008 ● 760-555-1212 ● John.Smith123@gmail.com ●
https://www.linkedin.com/in/johnsmith123

## Employment Coordinator

I am a professional Job Search Coach and Career Advisor assisting individuals to find their ideal career position. I have developed systems which enable people to accomplish their objectives in less time and with a minimal amount of effort. This is accomplished by utilizing repetition and repurposing of materials, processes, and assets. This methodology is more efficient and effective and yields better results in less time.

I have experience coordinating teams and training individuals in a variety of skills. I lead workshops for job seekers and provide individual coaching to assist professionals in advancing their careers. I have recruited and managed volunteers for organizations focused on assisting foster youth and families in transition between permanent housing.

I am a published author on topics ranging from careers, marketing real estate and leisure time activities.

## Skills

- In-depth knowledge of the job search process and experience coaching individuals and groups to be more effective in obtaining their next career position.

- Published author of articles detailing best practices in the fields of career advancement, employment and staffing, marketing, real estate and sports.

- Developing, growing and maintaining relationships with my external partner teams and our customer's senior executives.

- Planning, scheduling, budgeting and maintaining current and accurate employee databases using tools such as Google and Microsoft Office Productivity tools.

- The ability to clearly articulate product and service features and benefits in the context of customer requirements.

- Able to quickly analyze complex issues and take decisive action toward resolving them.

# Experience

**Director**
**Employment Assistance      Job Search Coaching and Assistance      2016 – Present**

- Assist individuals with their job search process utilizing a proprietary system which incorporates skills and techniques employed by sales professionals.
- Conduct job search workshops for foster youth, families in transition between permanent housing and other groups who would benefit from finding full-time employment.
- Publish articles about job search techniques, methods, and best practices. These were featured in a variety of electronic publications, on other job search websites and in social media.

**Managed Services Sales**
**Hardware Provider, Inc.      Reseller of IT Products and Services      2015 – 2016**

- Developed a new business program to expand the company's offerings and migrate the revenue sources from products to services, which resulted in higher margins per sale.
- Trained the sales staff in new services offerings and the selling strategies and techniques for services vs. products. The expanded the skill sets of the sales force and resulted in additional revenues per client.
- Recruited new vendor partners and integrated them into the company's sales portfolio thereby expanding the revenue streams available to the sales force.

**Account Executive**
**Computer Services Support      IT Maintenance and Services Provider      2009 – 2015**

- Consistently increased revenues and exceeded goals year over year by focusing my efforts and those of my partner teams on cross selling and up selling to existing clients.
- Recruited partners to help promote my organization's programs across other US geographies. Trained the partners and assisted them in rolling out the programs.
- Positioned myself as a consulting resource for my clients and guided them through the process of selecting the right solutions for their organization.
- Established revenue objectives, ensured the virtual team understood them and provided the support and resources required by the team to exceed the organization's goals.
- Increased the skill sets and results achieved by the organization and partner teams through regular training and coaching.
- Participated on committees which upgraded internal company tools including the CRM system and the client portal.

## Education

**Master's Degree, Business Administration**
1984 – 1986   San Diego State University / Marketing Department, San Diego, CA
Maintained 3.8 GPA and graduated in top 5% of my class.

**Bachelor's Degree, Business**
1977 – 1981   University of Kansas, School of Business, Lawrence, KS
Attained a BA in Business in a self-directed degree titled "Technical Sales."  This combined courses from the disciplines of Business, Chemistry, Physics, and Mathematics.

## Personal

- Married 30 Years, 2 Adult Children
- Board of Directors, Charitable Foundation
- Volunteer for organizations which provide assistance to foster children, homeless families and other people undergoing life challenges
- Interests include Flying, Diving, Surfing, Fishing, Golf, Travel

# Cover Letters

---

*"Hello/ I Love You/ Let me jump in your Game." – Jim Morrison*

---

T his famous lyric from the Doors summarizes the essence of a cover letter related to your job search process. You are trying to grab the attention of the hiring manager, get them to read your resume, and invite you to an interview. To be successful at this, you must accomplish 4 objectives with the cover letter:

1. Let them know why you are contacting them (Introduction)

2. Show them that you have taken the time to learn about them and their organization. Also, describe what attracts you to them (Flattery)

3. Summarize your qualifications to make you stand out (Brag)

4. Suggest the next steps in the process (Call to Action)

By following this model, you are more likely to capture the attention of the reader. Your cover letter needs to prompt them to at least read your resume, and ideally invite you in for an interview.

## Cover Letter Layout

### Introduction

The first section of the cover letter is the "Introduction." It should be a paragraph describing why you have contacted them and what position interests you. It is imperative to include a statement to describe your enthusiasm for the position and summarize your qualifications.

An example of this is:

> I am writing to express my interest in joining Acme's Logistics Organization in the role of Logistics Manager. I am excited about the opportunity to join such a prestigious organization as Acme, and I believe my skills and experience will be of benefit to you.

## Flattery – Talk about Them

The next section of the cover letter is the "Flattery" paragraph. This describes in two to three sentences what attracts you to their organization, citing characteristics of their company that resonate with you. It ends with a sentence which links the values of the organization to your personal values, thereby creating a connection between you and them.

Here is an example of this section of the cover letter:

> What attracts me to Acme is your wide selection of financial services and products. Your commitment to helping people and businesses reach their full potential is inspirational. You are well-known as a leader in your industry and your recent award for excellence from the industry trade group is evidence of this. It is no secret that your team has a reputation for being open and caring, and these characteristics match my personal values.

Another benefit of this section is that it demonstrates that you have taken the time to do some research and learn about their organization. This will set you apart from the many other applicants and let the reader know that this is not another "form" letter which most people use.

## Brag – Talk about You

The third section of the cover letter describes your experience, skills, and talents. The point is to convince the hiring manager that you qualify for the position. While the cover letter may not directly result in an interview, it should at least prompt them to read your resume to learn more about you. In this section., it is critical to use keywords and terminology listed in the job posting. This will help the reader create a connection between you with the position they are trying to fill. Here is an example of the "Brag" paragraphs:

> I believe I can bring a great deal of enthusiasm to your company and become a valued asset based on my portfolio of skills and experience working with individuals and businesses similar to your clients. Some of my qualifications include:

- 20+ years of advanced experience in logistics, distribution, transportation & supply chain management
- History of streamlining transportation operations, thereby saving millions of dollars
- Experience negotiating favorable rates of up to 30% off for services from suppliers
- Knowledge of how to develop efficient operational standards preferred by customers
- The ability to conduct strategic planning, resource allocation, leadership, production methods, and people/resource coordination

My background has helped me develop many personal qualities. I am enthusiastic, compassionate, and have a great sense of humor. These are just a few of my personality traits that will help me to contribute to the customer-oriented culture and strong work ethic your company is known for.

## Call to Action

The final section of your cover letter is a "call to action." It suggests what the hiring manager should do to move this process forward. This section is important because not only does it describe what you would like to see happen next, but it places you on par with the hiring manager. You do this by indicating that you are evaluating their company just like they are evaluating you. Most job candidates skip this part in their cover letter, so it will set you apart from the other applicants. The paragraph can read like the following:

> I recommend we arrange a time for a conversation, so we can explore whether Acme and I are a good fit for each other.
>
> Thank you for your time and consideration.
>
> Sincerely,
> First & Last Name
> Enclosure: Resume

Including these key points in your cover letter shows that you have taken the time to learn about their organization and you qualify for the position you are applying for. Once you have written your first cover letter using this format, you can easily edit it for other positions. All you need to do is update the information relevant to the organization you are applying to, and the position. As always, highlight your experience and skills which demonstrate your qualifications for this specific opportunity.

By following these recommendations and this structure for a cover letter, you are more likely to convince the hiring manager that you are serious about working for their organization. This will provide them the motivation to review your resume. If you have followed the guidelines for creating an effective resume and your qualifications match the requirements for the position, you are likely to get invited to an interview.

# Sample Cover Letter

November 30, 2017

Hiring Manager (Leave Blank if you don't know their name),

I am writing to express my interest in joining Acme's Logistics Organization in the role of Logistics Manager. I am excited about the opportunity to join such a prestigious organization as Acme, and I believe my skills and experience will be of benefit to you.

What attracts me to Acme is your wide selection of financial services and products. Your commitment to helping people and businesses reach their full potential is inspirational. You are well-known as a leader in your industry and your recent award for excellence from the industry trade group is evidence of this. It is no secret that your team has a reputation for being open and caring, and these characteristics match my personal values.

I believe I can bring a great deal of enthusiasm to your company and become a valued asset based on my portfolio of skills and experience working with individuals and businesses similar to your clients. Some of my qualifications include:

- 20+ years of advanced experience in logistics, distribution, transportation & supply chain management
- History of streamlining transportation operations, thereby saving millions of dollars
- Experience negotiating favorable rates of up to 30% off for services from suppliers
- Knowledge of how to develop efficient operational standards preferred by customers
- The ability to conduct strategic planning, resource allocation, leadership, production methods, and people/resource coordination

I recommend we arrange a time for a conversation, so we can explore whether Acme and I are a good fit for each other.

Thank you for your time and consideration.

Sincerely,

First & Last Name

Enclosure: Resume

# LinkedIn Profile

---

*"Invisible threads are the strongest ties." - Friedrich Nietzsche*

---

Friedrich Nietzsche probably never had a LinkedIn profile, or any other social media account for that matter since he lived in the 19th century. But, he knew that relationships were a key element of our personal and professional lives. Anything we can accomplish individually multiplies when we leverage the power of synergy and multiple people working together toward a common objective. This is true of your job search efforts.

The best online tool to create synergy and connections with other professionals in your field is LinkedIn. This social media site is specifically designed for business and can put you in touch with people who can advance your career. It functions as a digital version of your resume. Think of it as your personal website without the need to pay someone to create the site, host it, update it and post regular blogs.

To take full advantage of the power of LinkedIn and what it can do for you, there are some guidelines you need to follow. These fall into three categories;

1. Creating a compelling and informative profile
2. Connecting with other LinkedIn members in an effective and professional manner
3. Being active on the site to increase the number of views of your profile and the connection requests you receive

# Creating Your LinkedIn Profile

The easiest way to create or update your LinkedIn profile is to start at the top and work your way down through the profile in a systematic and organized manner. As with your resume, the most important part of your profile is near the top of the page. This will make the first impression on the people who are searching for you and will provide them the most information in the least amount of time.

To update your profile, select the pull-down menu underneath your picture in the black menu bar at the top of the page. Click on "View Profile." Your profile will now appear on the LinkedIn page. You can edit each section by clicking on the pencil icon.

## Photo

The first thing most people will see on your profile page is your picture. You should use a simple headshot showing you from the shoulders up. It goes without saying that you should be neatly groomed and dressed in business attire. It is best if you can use a picture taken by a professional photographer. However, any good clear headshot will do. CAUTION: do not use a selfie! If you need to use a picture taken with your phone, have someone else help you. If you have any questions about this simply log into LinkedIn and locate some other profile pictures that you find appealing and copy their format.

## Banner

The next thing you want to update is the banner photo behind your profile picture. This will help differentiate you from other people on LinkedIn. If you do not already have a banner photo in mind, I would recommend using a picture which reflects your profession or industry. You can also use a skyline picture from the city in which you live. You can find these by searching the Internet for Your "Profession", "Industry" or "City" followed by "Images." Save the picture to your computer and then upload it to LinkedIn using the editing tool.

## Headline

Moving down the page, you will next edit your headline. Most people's headlines simply reflect their most recent job title. However, since this is the second section people read, you can use it to explain what you are good at or how you can help them. You can use a series of titles which describe your role with your current employer, or you can use your professional title followed by a description of what you do. Here are some simple examples of good compelling headlines:

> **"Career Advisor and Job Search Coach, assisting professionals to advance their careers using creative strategies."**

> **"Sales Executive – Business Development Manager – New Client Acquisition Specialist – Revenue Generator"**

Your headline is an opportunity to begin to sell yourself. First do so as a potential employee. Then, after a company hires you, you can use it to connect with your clients or the people you want to network with. You should update your headline as is appropriate based on what you are trying to achieve with your LinkedIn page.

The next two sections at the top of the page are filled in by default, based on your employment history and education. Make sure that these accurately reflect your current position and the highest level of education you have attained.

The same is true for your location. It should reflect either where you currently reside or where you would like to work.

You can update the industry section using the drop-down menu. Again, this can reflect either what you currently do and have done in the past or what you are aspiring to do.

## Summary Statement

The next section at the top of the page is your summary statement. This is as important as your headline. People who are seriously interested in learning about you will take the time to scroll down and open this section of your profile. It is your opportunity to expand on your headline and give them details about what you do, your skills and experience, and how these can benefit them.

The easiest way to complete your summary section is to cut and paste the section from your resume. As discussed earlier, your resume summary should describe the same things noted above and reflect the title of your current position or the one you would like to obtain. Since your LinkedIn profile is your online resume, anytime you update your resume you should also update your LinkedIn profile. This would include your headline, the summary section, and your work experience.

The only caveat to using the same summary statement as your resume is that LinkedIn will only display the first 235 characters of your summary statement. Therefore, it is extremely important to make this impactful. This should not simply be a restatement of your work title or how much experience you have. It should be a strong statement telling the reader what value you bring and how you can help them resolve some issues or eliminate a pain they are experiencing. Once you have written this, it may be a good idea to revisit the summary statement in your resume to see if this opening sentence will work for that as well.

Another good idea is to put your contact information (email and phone number) in your summary statement. Many people are unfamiliar with LinkedIn and may not know where to locate your contact information. (Note, it is on the upper right side of your profile, adjacent to your summary section.) This will allow people to contact you directly without having to message you our use an InMail message if they are not already connected to you on LinkedIn.

If possible, try to include some media below your summary statement. This may be a copy of your resume, a link to your personal website, an example of some work you have done, or anything else that will provide the reader with some additional information about your skills, experience, and talent. If you are not sure what to upload, click on the "Supported Formats" link on the page. It will provide you some samples of providers that are compatible with this section of your profile.

## Experience

The next section of your LinkedIn profile details your experience. This too can be taken directly from your resume, if the resume is up to date and is written as discussed above. If you have multiple positions listed both on your resume and in your LinkedIn profile, you can begin to minimize or reduce the amount of information you provide for older positions. Employers and customers are more interested in what you have done recently. Older positions tend to reiterate your current experience or discuss skills which are no longer relevant to your career aspirations. Also, it is unlikely that most readers will get past the top three-to-four job positions you describe.

## Education

After people review your work experience, the next thing they are interested in is your education. This too can be copied directly from your resume. When you include the college or institution you have attended, use the formal name so that their logo appears on your profile. (Note, this is true for your professional experience as well.) This makes for a more attractive LinkedIn profile and will encourage people to connect with you. The degree stated in the education section should contain both the initials and the full description. An example would be *MBA, Masters of Business Administration.* This will make your profile easier to find by search engines and Applicant Tracking Systems (ATS.) Another tip is to briefly describe something unique about your educational experience or to list some major accomplishments during this period. This will help distinguish you from other LinkedIn profiles.

## Optional Sections

Once you have completed the educational section of your LinkedIn profile, you have several optional sections you can insert. You do this by going back to the top of the page and opening the "Add new profile section." Options listed here include Volunteer Experience, Skills, and Accomplishments. Under Accomplishments, you will see options including Publications, Certifications, Projects, and Honors & Awards. You should complete as many of these as possible, as long as the information you list is relevant to the position you are looking to obtain. The writing style of these items should be brief and concise. Each item should contain a descriptive title, the dates the item was performed or accomplished, and a brief description of the contributions made, or the honors received.

## Skills

A special note about the Skills section. This part of your LinkedIn profile allows you to choose a list of skills associated with your employment and educational experience. Once a list is in your profile, your LinkedIn connections can endorse you for each of these skills. Most people with LinkedIn profiles will list as many skills as possible, and not necessarily in the correct order. Even though they may receive multiple endorsements for each of the skills, employers discount these. Employers know that people will endorse each other without any real knowledge of the other person's capabilities or skill sets.

A better strategy for this section is to list 12-to-15 key skills, placing the most relevant ones for the job you are seeking at the top the list. LinkedIn only displays the top three skills, so make sure these are the ones you want people to be aware of. Even if you don't have endorsements for these (yet,) they will still make an impact on an employer.

## Recommendations

Below the Featured Skills and Endorsements section, there is a place where people can provide recommendations for you. You cannot fill out this section yourself, but there are ways that you can get people to provide you recommendations. The easiest, the most direct way is to ask. Reach out to some of your close associates who are on LinkedIn requesting that they write a brief recommendation for you to help you obtain your next professional position. You may even want to draft a simple example of a recommendation, then suggest that your connection edit this to fit their own words and writing style. People are generally happy to help you if they respect your skills, qualifications, and are genuinely interested in assisting you to get your next position. Make sure that the request is not intrusive or demanding and that you only ask for a recommendation once. If they do not respond, move on to one of your other LinkedIn connections. However, if they do provide you with a recommendation, make sure that 1.) You thank them and 2.) You provide them with a corresponding recommendation on their profile.

Another less direct method to get a recommendation is to give a recommendation. Proactively provide recommendations for some of your LinkedIn connections that you know well and who are able to provide you with a recommendation. This takes approximately 5 to 10 minutes and is something you can easily do once a day.

When recommending somebody, write 3-4 sentences which describe your relationship with the person, some of their work habits and accomplishments that you admire, and a recommendation for somebody to either work with them or hire them.

The following is a sample of a new recommendation or a colleague:

> Mike and I worked together at Our Company in a variety of capacities and I have continued to follow Mike's career since then. He is a consummate professional and excels at everything he does for the organizations he works for. Much of this is due to his dedication to customer satisfaction and simultaneous focus on the business objectives of the organization. He is able to connect these factors in a manner that benefits both parties. Mike is highly thought of by his clients, business associates, and coworkers. He brings his casual demeanor and sense of humor into the workplace. He is attentive to details, driven to succeed and has a strong work ethic. Mike would be a great asset to any business organization.

Ideally, you would like to have a minimum of 4-6 well-written recommendations on your profile. More is better, but you don't need dozens. Your profile will also show how many recommendations you have provided to your other LinkedIn connections. The number given should not exceed the number received by more than 50%, or it will look like you have been "fishing" for recommendations.

## Accomplishments

The next section of your LinkedIn profile is a description of your accomplishments. These can include:

- Publications
- Certifications
- Courses you have taken in addition to your formal Education
- Projects you have completed
- Honors and Awards you have received
- Patents
- Languages you speak
- Organizations you belong to

Like all the other sections of your LinkedIn profile, the items you list in this section and the details you provide should be relevant to your career advancement objective. Listing too many items or accomplishments that are insignificant or unrelated to your career will detract from the major accomplishments. These may get lost in the "noise."

## Interests

The final section of your LinkedIn profile is a collection of your interests. These include your Influencers, Companies, Groups, and Schools you follow on LinkedIn. This section provides a potential employer with a complete picture of you, your background and what you do outside of work. It is important to make sure these are professional, relevant and informative.

Influencers are industry luminaries, thought leaders and individuals whose business or personal philosophies have helped shaped you into the person you are. The added benefit of following Influencers on LinkedIn is that their posts will show up on your homepage. This enables you to continue to learn from their experience and wisdom.

To follow an Influencer, simply search for them on LinkedIn and then click on the "Follow" button located on the Menu Icon (⋯) on the right side of their profile.

You can follow Companies and Schools the same way you follow Influencers and using the same criteria.

Groups are different from the other categories of your Interests. Being a member of LinkedIn Groups is an effective way to grow your network, increase your influence and attract views to your profile. Groups and how to leverage them in your job search strategy are discussed in the next section.

# Using LinkedIn for Your Job Search and Career Advancement

---

*"Don't be mysterious. It is the last resort of people with no secrets." Maggie Smith*

---

Most jobs (some estimates are as high as 80%) are obtained through referrals from people who you know or who are aware of your background. Therefore, the most effective way to get a job is to leverage your business connections. The easiest way to expand your business connections is by using LinkedIn.

Here are some actions you can take to;

- Locate companies and individuals on LinkedIn
- Increase your professional network by connecting with LinkedIn members and starting a conversation with them
- Increase the number of views of your LinkedIn profile so you start receiving connection requests and invitations to interview

# Searching on LinkedIn

The LinkedIn search bar at the top of every page allows you to search for people, jobs, companies, posts, and more. You can click any of the search suggestions that appear in the dropdown list as you type, or submit your search to see the full results.

### Running a Search

To run a search on LinkedIn:

1. Enter your keyword in the search bar at the top of your page.
2. Once you have entered your keyword into the search bar, select from the drop-down menu to search for jobs, people, groups or other categories that appear based on your keyword.
3. Click Search.

4. On the search results page, you will see the following tabs at the top of your page:
- Top
- People
- Jobs
- Groups
- Schools
5. Select any of the tabs to view search results in that category.

**Note:** You will be able to apply search filters, such as locations and connections, from the Top search results tab.

## Finding a specific person

To find a specific person:

If you know the first and last name, type it into the search bar. You can also search for first and last name using the Keyword filters found on the right rail of the Top and People search results tabs. For example:

- Richard Branson

You can also include keywords such as company or job title. For example:

- Richard Branson Virgin Group
- Richard Branson Founder

If you don't know their full name, enter other information that you know about them. For example:

- President, Virgin Group

To search for multiple people, type your search criteria into the search bar. For example:

- Manager Internships Australia

After submitting a search, click the **People** tab at the top of the search results page.

You can narrow down your search by applying the filters on the right of the page.

## Finding a Specific Company or Multiple Companies

To find a specific company or multiple companies:

If you know the company's name, type it into the search box. For example:

- Virgin Airline

If you don't know the name, enter a partial name and/or characteristic of the company that may be associated with the Company Page. For example:

- Virgin travel
- Budget Flights

To search for multiple companies, type your search criteria into the search box. For example:

- Flights from Melbourne to Sydney

Click the Companies tab at the top of the page to view all companies that fall within your search criteria.

When searching in LinkedIn, remember to be patient. It may take several searches to locate the information you are trying to find. Also, be creative. Start with specific search terms and broaden these, removing descriptive adjectives until you begin to get results. After several searches, you will become proficient at this and subsequent searches will be easier.

# Growing your Network

Having a large network of connections on LinkedIn is the best way to leverage this social media site to market yourself and find a job. Not only will you be able to communicate with your direct LinkedIn connections, but you can see who they are connected to. You can use this to send those people a connection request or ask your current connection for an introduction to them. Once you are connected with someone, you can begin a conversation about your career goals.

Invitations to connect are an essential tool to help you grow your professional network and make meaningful connections. There is a right way and a wrong way to send someone a LinkedIn Connection request.

## Inviting or Connecting with People on LinkedIn

You can ask someone to join your professional network by sending them an invitation to connect. If they accept your invitation, they will become a 1st-degree connection.

You can invite people to connect from:

- A member's profile: Click the Connect button on their profile page, then click on "Add a note."

- Search results: Click Connect to the right of the person's information.
- The Grow Your Network page: Search your email address book to find contacts or invite them using their email address.
- The People You May Know page: Click the person's name, then click on the Connect button on the right side of their profile.

## Personalizing Invitations to Connect

When inviting members to connect, you should always add a personalized message to the recipient to introduce yourself or add context to your relationship.

To add a message to an invitation:

1. Visit the member's profile page and click Connect.
2. Click Add a note.
3. Add your message in the text field.
4. Click Send Invitation.

Here is an example of a personalized LinkedIn Connection Message:

> Julie, I would like to connect with you on LinkedIn. Since we are both active in the staffing business I am sure a relationship would be mutually beneficial. My regular posts about HR topics on LinkedIn may be of interest to you. Thanks for your consideration. Bill

If the recipient replies to your message, you will receive an email to the account associated with your LinkedIn profile and it will also appear in your LinkedIn messaging.

## Inviting People Using Their Individual Email Address

To invite people using their email address:

1. Click the My Network icon at the top of your homepage.
2. Click More Options on the left side of the page.
3. Click Invite by email on the right side of the page.
4. Type the email addresses, separated by commas, into the text box on the left.
5. Click Continue.

Note: Invitations sent this way cannot be personalized.

## Starting a Conversation

Starting a conversation with a new LinkedIn connection is easy. You send your new connection a brief message with some of the following components.

- Thank them for connecting.

- Let them know why you wanted to connect with them.
- Offer to assist them (minimally you can offer to introduce them to your other LinkedIn connections.)
- Ask them for their assistance if you need it, but do it briefly and politely. Don't ask a second time if they don't respond, just move on to another contact.

Here is an example of a "Thank You" message to someone who has accepted your LinkedIn Invitation:

> Madison, Thanks for accepting my connection request on LinkedIn. Let me know if I can help you with anything or introduce you to any of my other LinkedIn associates. Bill

If they reply, even with a simple "Thanks", then you can continue the conversation. One easy thing to do is to scan their other connections and ask them to introduce you to one of them. Let them know why you would like to connect with the other individual. You can use this opportunity to politely introduce the fact that you are in the job search process and would appreciate it if they would introduce you to one of their other connections.

Here is an example of this type of message.

> Mike, I notice that you are connected to Richard Branson at Virgin Group. Would it be possible for you to send Richard a brief introduction to me? I am currently looking for other employment and am interested in exploring opportunities with Virgin. Thanks in advance for your assistance with this. Bill

## Connecting with Prospects within Target Companies

To Follow Companies

- Search for the companies you want to work for by selecting Companies in the pull-down menu to the left of the "Search" field at the top of your LinkedIn page. Type the Company name and hit the search button.
- Hit "Follow" if you are not already following them.

To Connect with Individuals within Prospect Companies

- Hit View so see the company profile
- Hit See all employees on LinkedIn ->
- Any employee listed with "Connect" next to their name can be sent a connection request by clicking on the button. As mentioned before, it is better to send a note with the connection request.

- Use this selectively and only send connection requests to 3-4 contacts initially. Select contacts by using the titles which are most frequently associated with the Hiring Managers for the positions you are interested in.
- Once you get some responses, you can send a few more connection requests; one for every new confirmation you receive back is a good rule to work by.

Repeat this for each company you are interested in.

### Accepting a Request

As you become more active on LinkedIn and start to be proactive about increasing the number of views of your Profile, you will begin receiving Connection Requests. Accepting these in a proper manner will demonstrate your professionalism and lead you to the possibility of generating employment opportunities via LinkedIn. Here are the steps in the process of accepting a connection request effectively.

- You will receive an email notifying you of a connection request. Simply click on the "Accept" button and it will direct you to LinkedIn.
- Always send a message to a new connection after accepting their connection request. The message should thank them for inviting you to connect and offer to help them in any way you can, such as introducing them to some of your other contacts.

Here is a sample message when accepting a LinkedIn Connection Request:

> Jack, Thanks for inviting me to connect with you on LinkedIn. I am happy to make your acquaintance and look forward to following you and learning more about the work you and your organization do. Let me know if there is anything I can help you with or anyone else on LinkedIn you would like me to introduce you to. Bill

Once you are connected with someone on LinkedIn, you can message them using the "Send a message" link. NOTE: This is not an InMail message and does not require a Premium membership.

# Groups

Being a member of a group provides you with access to many more LinkedIn members without having a formal connection or relationship with them on LinkedIn. You can message other members of groups, post items of specific interest to the group and start conversations. These latter two actions will help to increase your profile views and may result in additional LinkedIn connection requests. (See Increasing Your Profile Views for more information on this topic.)

Here are the steps to find and join LinkedIn Groups

- Type the Company or Industry name and hit the search button.
- Search for the groups affiliated with companies you want to work with. Select Groups in the pull-down menu below the Search field at the top of your LinkedIn page.
- Select the Group you would like to join.

Once you are a member of a group, you can leverage this to increase the views of your profile and make additional connections. More on this later.

# Increasing your Profile Views on LinkedIn

One of the easiest ways to leverage LinkedIn as a job search tool is to increase the number of people who are viewing your profile on the site. This will generate more connection requests, thus expanding your network. It will also encourage people to learn more about what you do so they will inquire about your employment availability status. They are also more likely to refer you to one of their other LinkedIn connections.

## Profile Keywords

The first thing you need to do to increase the views of your profile is to leverage keywords and phrases in your profile so people searching on these terms will find you. This was already discussed in the section about creating your profile. Take a minute to review this section.

## Groups

Another way to increase your profile views on LinkedIn is to be an active member of groups related to your employment objectives. How to locate and join groups was previously discussed. Here is how to leverage your membership in the groups to increase your profile views and generate interest in your products and services.

There are three main ways to use a membership in a group to increase your profile views:

- Connection Invitations and Messages to other group members
- Starting Conversations within the group forum
- Posting to the Group Page

## Connections & Messages

Once you are a member of a group, you can use LinkedIn's search and messaging features to locate other LinkedIn Group members, invite them to connect with you, and/or send them a message. The guidelines mentioned for sending connection invitations and messaging in the main part of LinkedIn applies to the Groups section as well. The key is, "Be Brief, Be Bright and Be Gone." A polite message stating your reason for contacting another LinkedIn member and the benefits you offer them works best. If they do not respond, don't continue to contact them. They are either not interested in your offering or they do not actively use LinkedIn. This is OK. There are millions of LinkedIn members so just move on to someone else who may be interested in connecting with you. If they do respond, then start a conversation with them utilizing the guidelines already provided.

## Conversations

Another effective method to use LinkedIn Groups to increase views of your profile is to start a conversation within the Group forum. Not only does this publish your name and a connection to your profile when you start the conversation, but it puts your profile at the top of the conversation each time another member of the group comments or responds to it. The more activity from the group, the more often your profile appears in the Group forum section.

The key to a Group Conversation is to make it topical, relevant and interesting. You can start a conversation by asking an interesting, contemporary or thought-provoking question which other group members will respond to. Another way to begin a conversation is by posting a connection to an article about a topic of interest to the group and then encourage comments.

Either of these conversations starts by going to the Group Page, then simply posting in the "Start a Conversation with your Group" section. You create an eye-catching title, ask a question or provide a link to a post on a topic and/or upload a file. It is very easy and only takes a few minutes.

Some general guidelines for using Conversations in the Group pages:

- Do not use a conversation to promote yourself as this is not an advertising tool. You can share a link to a blog or white paper posted on your personal or company site. But, it should be relative to the title of the conversation and the introduction you provided.

- Avoid controversial topics:
    - Politics
    - Religion
    - Sports
- Don't use the discussion to criticize or defame other individuals or organizations within the group or the industry affiliated with it.
- Only start 1-2 conversations per week so you can both manage the conversations by replying to other people who join the conversation. This prevents you from becoming become "noise" to other members of the group.

Another way to use the Conversations in a LinkedIn Group page is to comment on or contribute to other people's conversations. This will put your comments and a link to your profile at the top of the conversation, just under the conversation creator's link. Commenting on a conversation may also lead to a dialog with the conversation creator or one of the other participants.

When commenting on someone else's conversation, follow the general guidelines. Keep your comments professional, respectful and germane to the topic of the conversation. This will help to establish you as a subject matter expert and attract other people to want to connect with you.

**Posts**

Posting to a Group page is another way to increase your visibility on LinkedIn. Posts are different than conversations in that they are one-time events. They usually involve original content or a link to something relevant to the group. Other people can "Like", "Comment" or "Share" the post which does increase the visibility of the post on LinkedIn, but not as often as responses to a conversation will.

You post to a Group the same way to post to your profile on LinkedIn, but you designate the post for the Group. It will then show up on both your profile and on the Group page. Posting is discussed next.

# Posting on LinkedIn

Another way to increase the views of your profile on LinkedIn is to Post information on your profile. You can do this in a matter of a few minutes and don't have to create original content to post. You can search the internet for articles, news, and resources related to your skills and expertise and post the link to these on LinkedIn. Once you do this a few times, you will learn how to create a LinkedIn post in less than five minutes.

## Original Content

Posting original content is the best way to get people to connect with you and regularly visit your profile. Since the content is unique to you and others can only find it on your page, this sets you apart from other prospective employees in your industry. However, creating original content is time-consuming. You can and should author original content if you have the talent to do so, but there are alternatives to this. Some companies have social media specialists who are responsible for creating content for the company's web page and other social media sites. Most employers will encourage you to repurpose this content. Posting this content on your LinkedIn page will increase its visibility.

## Third Party Content

If you either do not have the time or the skills to create original content or do not want to post your organization's posts, then the easiest way to add content to your LinkedIn page is to repurpose other content already on the internet or posted on LinkedIn. This is an efficient way to establish yourself as a subject matter expert. It is completely legal if you acknowledge the original source of the content in the post. In fact, most content creators encourage this because it expands the audience for their material.

## How to Post

There are two ways to post content on LinkedIn; Sharing and Posting.

### Shared Content

Sharing is easier, but not as effective. Shared content is labeled as such and may also be shared multiple times by other LinkedIn members, thereby diluting its impact. Simply sharing content will not get you as many views, followers and connections requests as original content or content obtained outside of LinkedIn.

To share content, simply click on the "Share" button below the post. This will open a new window with the original post and space for you to add a comment. You should comment so that you others perceive you to have some expertise on the subject of the post.

### External Content

Content obtained outside of LinkedIn is easier to post than original content and can be just as effective in increasing your LinkedIn visibility. The key is to find interesting information relevant to your target audience and to post it in an appropriate manner.

Finding content is as easy as searching for keywords related to your skills or expertise using any search engine. Once you locate an interesting article or link, you can post it two ways: Using a LinkedIn Share button embedded with the content or by copying the URL of the page where the content is located.

**LinkedIn Share Button**

Clicking on the LinkedIn Share button on the page where the content is located will open a window which shows you what the post will look like. This allows you to select a relevant image to accompany the post and enable you to add a comment to the post. Commenting on the post is critical because this allows you to customize the post to make it relevant to your career. You can even add a "call to action" by suggesting the reader contact you if they find the post interesting and would like to speak in more detail about your expertise in the topic discussed in the post.

**Content URL**

You can post using the content URL by:

1. Copying the URL in the search bar of your browser.
2. Open your LinkedIn Homepage and click on the "Share an article, photo or update" box in the middle of the top of the page.
3. Paste the URL into this section. This will show the top of the article and possibly an image or selection of images you can choose from.
4. Add your comment, introduction or call to action to the comment section in the top of the box.
5. Click on the "Post" button to post the article on your profile.

Once you post., the article will show up on your connections LinkedIn home page with a set of buttons to "Like", "Comment" or "Share." You will be notified in your "Notifications" section if someone takes one of these actions.

The guidelines for Posts are the same as those for conversations, except for the frequency. You can post daily, but only once per day. Three to four times per week is the most effective frequency to remain relevant and not become "noise."

## Conclusion

The key to an effective LinkedIn profile is not only having a well written and organized profile, but also leveraging the tool to make connections and be viewed by other LinkedIn members. This requires consistent effort, utilizing proven methods which get you the results you are looking for in either your job search or your current job.

# Locating Prospective Employers and Hiring Managers

---

*"The voyage of discovery is not in looking for new landscapes, but in looking with new eyes." —Anonymous*

---

Once you have developed your job search collateral materials (resume, cover letter, and LinkedIn profile) it is time to figure out who you are going to send them to. These will be potential employers who meet your job search strategy criteria:

- The Job Title
- Description of the Duties
- Requirements needed to obtain the position, including
  - Education
  - Experience
  - Skill Set
- Target Industry
- Geography
- Income you require

Depending on what stage of your career you are at, you may already know who these companies and/or hiring manager contacts are. These may be companies and individuals already in your network if you have been working for a while. If you are just starting out, you may need to do a lot of research to locate your target employers. Either way, you will need to develop a list of target employers and a plan to send them your resume in the hope of getting an interview for a job.

# Networking

The best and most effective way to locate potential employers is to tap your network of personal and professional connections. Studies show that 80% of hires are due to a personal referral. This is the most effective and efficient way to locate employers who have positions open which match your qualifications. Many organizations have programs which reward their employees for referrals of potential candidates who are subsequently hired by the company. Additionally, people are usually proud of where they work and are anxious to have their friends and business acquaintances join the company.

There is a right way and a wrong way to leverage the people you know to help you get a job. The right way is to simply inform them that you are in the process of searching for your next job and provide a summary of what type of position that interests you. You can do this in several ways. The best and easiest is to bring it up during a normal conversation. Just about any interaction between two people, either professional or personal, starts with a question like "So, how are you?" or "What's new?" or "What have you been up to?" This is a perfect opening to provide a brief, high-level description of your job search activity and objective. If the other person responds and offers their assistance or some suggestions as to where you may find an employment opportunity, Great! If not, then move on to other topics of discussion. Even if they don't offer to help you, they are now aware of your situation and will recognize an opportunity for you if it comes to their attention. It is like when you get a new car. All the sudden you see dozens of the same model in places that you have never seen them before.

Another, more direct method to make your network of acquaintances aware of your quest to find a new job is to send them an email informing them of your situation. Ask them to keep their eyes open for opportunities which fit your skills and experience. While this method is a little more invasive than simply having a conversation about your job search, if done properly it can be effective. Do not ask your contacts for direct assistance or to forward your resume to a hiring manager. Simply make them aware that you are in the process of searching for a job so that they will be alert to any opportunities that come along which may fit your portfolio of skills and experience.

The third and final way to leverage your network to find employment opportunities is to follow the guidelines detailed in the chapter about LinkedIn. Using your network of LinkedIn contacts, the groups you belong to, and companies you follow, you can tactfully make them aware that you are in the job search process. This will get your profile exposed to multiple opportunities which may lead to an interview offer.

# LinkedIn

As discussed earlier, LinkedIn is a great resource when trying to locate prospective employers or hiring managers. You can refer to the section about searching on LinkedIn to learn how to target specific organizations and individuals. Once you have located the company you would like to work for and the prospective hiring manager, you can find their contact information using several different techniques.

The easiest way to locate a hiring manager's contact information on LinkedIn is simply to request a connection. Message them and let them know that you are interested in learning more about the company and the work they do. If they respond positively and confirm the connection, then you can politely send them a message with your resume suggesting that your skills and experience may be of some use to the company.

If a hiring manager you are trying to connect with on LinkedIn doesn't respond, there are other ways to locate their contact information. Determine if one of your current connections is connected with them. You can reach out to that person and ask them for the information you are looking for. Or you can request an introduction to the contact. If you are not connected to the hiring manager indirectly, look for other individuals who work for the company with whom you may have a common connection with. Seek out their contact information using the same methodology discussed above. Once you have this, you can reliably determine what the contact information for your prospective hiring manager is.

Most organizations use common conventions for their email address formats. These include

- **firstname.lastname@companyname.com**
- **firstinitiallastname@companyname.com**
- **firstnamelastinitial@companyname.com**

Smaller companies typically use the format of **firstname@companyname.com**. If you know the email address of one person within the company, you can typically extrapolate those of the other employees. You may not always be right, and if not, the email will bounce indicating that you need to try a different format. This simple trial and error methodology takes very little time and usually yields good results.

## Job Boards

Job boards are another way you can locate hiring managers. Often, the hiring manager for companies is listed on the job posting. If not, the posting may reference an email address for someone in the HR Department. Even though this is not the hiring manager, it is a good place to start. While it is always best to communicate directly with the hiring manager sometimes you must start with HR because there is no other option.

When using a job board to locate a specific hiring manager, search for multiple positions within the organization. Even if it is not an exact match for the department or the position that you are seeking, you can send an email to the contact you find and ask them to forward it to the appropriate person within the company for the job which you are interested in. The key is to be creative. Trying a variety of methods will eventually get you to the right person. Additionally, challenging yourself to find the right person using different techniques will add some fun and interest to your job search process.

# Online Databases

There are several online databases which list contacts and companies in a variety of industries and locations. The way many of these work is people upload their contact databases in exchange for points or credits which can then be used to search and download the other contacts' information. Normally there is an even exchange. You get a number of credits for each contact which you upload. You can then use the credits to purchase the information for the contact you want to communicate with.

There are some considerations when using these databases. First, you need to upload the complete and current information of your business contacts. This usually includes the first and last names, title, company name, phone number, and email address. Second, the contacts you upload should have freely given you their information as part of a business transaction. You should not upload a personal contact's information or information you acquired from another source without the contact's knowledge.

One of the ways you can use online databases to locate hiring manager's information is to simply purchase the information from the database. This does not require you to upload any information from your contact list. You simply pay a fee for each contact whose information you want from the database. The fees range from $2 to $10 per contact, so using this method can get very expensive very quickly. However, if you only need a few contact names and information, or you do not have an extensive database you can upload, this is an easy way to use the online database.

## Conclusion

Communicating directly with a hiring manager will always be more effective than "broadcasting" your job search via job boards or online job postings. Locating the hiring managers and finding their contact information is not difficult if you employ the same techniques professional sales people use when prospecting for clients.

# The Interview

---

*"Death will be a great relief. No more interviews." - Katherine Hepburn*

---

**K**atherine Hepburn summed up just about everyone's perception of job interviews in this quote. Next to death and public speaking, they are probably the most dreaded event in a person's life, or at least their professional life. However, a job interview can be easy and even pleasurable if you know how to execute one properly.

Many people worry about this step the most, considering it is the biggest challenge in the job search process. They are right. Your LinkedIn profile and cover letter got you noticed. Your resume got you in the door, but lots of people can write a good resume, especially with the help of guidelines provided by experts or by using a resume writing service. Now you need to ace the interview, and there is no one sitting next to you to help you do this. The key is to go into interviews well prepared, having a positive outlook and a clear focus on selling yourself as the best-qualified candidate. Interviews are key to an employer's decision to hire or not. Personality and presentation matter as much as the content of your answers to questions about your qualifications.

## Preparation

Most interviews are won or lost even before you walk through the door at the employer's office. If you are not properly prepared prior to the interview your chances of success are minimal. You will not be able to respond to the interviewer's questions properly, you will likely be nervous, and you may not make a good first impression due to being late. Also, being improperly dressed or ill-prepared for the logistics of the interview will hurt you in the long run. With a good preparation routine, you can be ready for any interview and go in with the confidence and knowledge that you will be able to do the best you possibly can.

The key elements of being prepared for a job interview are:

1. Research
2. Logistics
3. Questions
4. What to do during the interview
5. Follow up

By taking the time to address each of these areas before the actual interview, you will minimize the chance for any "surprises." You will be able to address any situation that normally would cause stress during an interview with poise and professionalism.

# Research

The best way to prepare for an interview and to build your confidence is to conduct a great deal of research prior to the meeting with the hiring manager. It is said that "Knowledge is Power," and the more you know going into the interview the more you will be in control of the conversation.

There are three areas you need to research prior to the interview:

1. The company
2. The position
3. The interviewer

The more you know about each one of these topics, the better prepared you will be to not only respond to the questions asked but to begin to take control of the interview by asking questions yourself. More about this later.

## The Company

The first focus of your pre-interview research is the company you are applying to. You have probably already done some work in this area while editing your resume and composing your cover letter. However, you now need to learn a lot more about the company than you already know. Ideally, you will be more familiar with all the aspects of the company than the person who is interviewing you and this will give you an advantage. You can frame your answers to the interviewer's questions in the context of the characteristics of the company. These include:

- Their Business Practices
- Business, Financial and Market Objectives
- Recent Financial Performance
- Market Challenges and Threats to their Business
- Competition

- Management Team
- Corporate History

These are the areas of the employer's business you need to explore and learn about.

During the interview, you want to demonstrate how you can help the company "make money, save money, save time (improving a process) and contribute to their corporate culture." The more you know about the company and the items listed above, the better you will be able to address your answers to their questions in the context of what contributions you can make. It will also allow you to prepare the questions you will be asking them, which is the most crucial part of the interview and how you will assume control of the interview process. This will be discussed later.

Sources for information about these aspects of the company's business include:

- The company's website
- A general internet search of the company's name
- Industry and Trade Association websites related to the company's products, services or market
- Government sites (if the company is publicly owned or otherwise regulated by the government)
- Job Boards such as Monster, Indeed and others
- LinkedIn
- Glassdoor.com, which provides reviews from current and previous employees

There are other internet sites you can search to learn more about the company, however, these will give you a good start.

You may also know people who work at the company you are applying to. Reaching out to your internal contacts is always recommended, but having them send you proprietary information is not. If the company learns you had advance knowledge of classified information or the interview questions, it will kill your chances of getting hired or impact your career after they hire you. There are other ways to accomplish this.

Go to glassdoor.com and search for the company. The site will provide information on the company, salary ranges for specific positions, reviews from current and former employees and descriptions of the interview process with some of the questions you should anticipate.

When conducting your research, make notes about significant achievements, events, or news about the company. Either print out information you find online or create a set of notes for review prior to the interview and which you can reference while you are being interviewed.

## The Position

Knowing as much as you can about the position will also help you during the interview. You will be able to address the requirements of the job when describing your prior experience, skill sets, knowledge and talents. You can also demonstrate to the interviewer how you will be able to contribute to the organization's business objectives and how the position you are seeking fits into the company's strategy to achieve their goals.

Sources for information about the position are like those you used to research the company. In addition to these, you can get information from the following:

• The original Job Posting
• Postings of similar jobs at other companies (Job Boards are the best source for these)
• A general internet search for the Position's Title
• Wikipedia

Again, you can reach out to contacts who are currently with the organization or who previously worked there. Ask your contacts about the people who are currently in the position you are applying for or ones who formerly were. You can then search for their LinkedIn Profiles to learn more about them. You can also go to an organization's LinkedIn page and try to find people who manage the position you are applying for or list the position in their profile as a former role. If you can, identify the hiring manager you will be interviewing with and see how they describe the role and what they or the previous job holders accomplished while in the position you are applying for.

Make notes of this information and bring it with you so you can review it prior to the meeting and refer to it during the interview.

## The Interviewer

Knowing as much as you can about the person or people you will be meeting with is very important to helping you succeed at the interview. We are all more comfortable talking with people we know than we are speaking with strangers, especially ones who can influence our career. The more you know about the interviewer or interviewers, the quicker you can build a rapport with them and move the interview from an "inquisition" to a "conversation."

The information you should seek about the people you will interview with is:

- Current Position with the company
- Tenure with the company
- Who they report to
- Former Positions (either with the company or with other organizations)
- Educational background
- Influencers
- Awards, Certifications, Acknowledgements
- Any personal information you can find including volunteer work, professional memberships, awards and recognitions, and interests and hobbies

Much of this information is available on LinkedIn, the company website, Facebook or by just "Googling" the interviewer's name and examining the search results.

Again, make notes of this information and bring it with you so you can review it prior to the meeting and refer to it during the interview.

# Logistics

Another key area you need to prepare for to have a successful outcome at an interview is the logistics. These are the details of when, where, with whom, how long and what next. Not being aware of the details in any one of these areas can result in failure no matter how well you have prepared for the other components of the interview. Conversely, spending some time preparing for the logistics will ensure you have a flawless experience. It will increase your confidence and will enable you to focus on the content of the interview.

## When & Where?

The location of the interview seems like it should be straightforward, but unanticipated issues may arise which could result in you either arriving late or, worse yet, going to the wrong location. A company may have several locations, a campus with multiple buildings, separate entrances for each part of the building or other issues that make it challenging to arrive at the right site and on time. There may be challenges with construction or other delays on-route to the location, parking issues and the need to pass through security checkpoints or fill out registration materials prior to meeting with the interviewer.

The best way to prepare for these is to ask the person who is arranging the interview about them. Confirm the address and ask for advice about parking and the appropriate building entrance. Inquire about security and filling out forms prior to the meeting. A company may require you to provide a photo ID or other documentation so ask about this as well.

Prior to the interview, visit the location at the same time as the scheduled interview to determine how long it will take to travel there. Note any potential delays such as traffic, construction or special events the day of the interview.

Once you determine the time it takes to get to the interview site from where you are staying, add thirty minutes. This will allow for unanticipated delays. It will also give you time to review your notes, reread your resume, and prepare yourself mentally if you end up arriving early.

## With Whom and for How Long?

It is important to know who you will be meeting with and how long you should plan to be at the company site. This will allow you to do your research on the interviewer or interviewers, and allow enough time in your schedule, so you do not feel rushed or need to terminate the interview early to get to another engagement. This information is easily obtained from the person who is responsible for scheduling the interview. It is better to ask about this prior to the interview than to be surprised when you arrive onsite.

## What Next?

Every interview is unique in terms of the process from start to finish. Some are brief, to the point and result in a decision while you are still in the interview. Others take days, weeks or even months. Some may even involve multiple interviews, site visits, tests or other types of screenings and activities. Knowing the process in advance will help you to better prepare for the next step and will also set the proper expectations for the meeting you are preparing for.

You may not always be able to find out the details of the interview process you are about to engage in, but it does not hurt to ask. The times you have the most leverage during the interview and hiring process is after they have invited you to come in for an interview but prior to the interview itself, and once you have received a job offer. These are the times you should use to gain as much information as possible and ask for any concessions you would like to receive. Knowing about the process before engaging in it is a reasonable request. If you meet resistance from the employer to provide you with at least a general description of their interview and hiring process, you may want to interpret this as a "red flag" and be wary of making any commitments which seem unusual.

# Questions

Another important area you need to prepare for is the questions you will be asked. Just as every job candidate is unique, so is every interviewer. Many organizations do not provide hiring managers with formal interview questions or training, so they will ask for information they feel is important. Some will seek to determine your level of knowledge about the job you are applying for. Others will be more interested in your previous experience and how you performed in positions like the one you are interviewing for. Some interviewers will even try to "trip you up" with unusual or unrelated questions just to see how you react. It is impossible to know the answer to every question that they may ask you.

## Tell me about yourself

While there is no way to anticipate and prepare for an answer to every question you may encounter, you can expect some general types of questions and be ready with appropriate responses. The first of these is, "Tell me about yourself." This is an icebreaker, allows the interviewer to learn some general information about you and is a jumping off point for the questions which follow.

This question enables you to make a positioning statement. The answer is usually the same as your "elevator pitch," which is a 30 second summary of your professional qualities and how you can contribute to an organization's business objectives. You can use the summary section of your resume as the basis for your response to this question.

Here is a sample of an answer to the "Tell me about yourself" question:

> I am an experienced Human Resources Professional, adept at selecting talent which meets the requirements of an organization's staffing needs in an efficient and effective manner. I have developed a screening system which resulted in shortened the time required to fill vacant positions and reduced new hire turnover by 20%. I am skilled at writing job descriptions and posting them to the appropriate social media and online job boards. I have trained hiring managers to conduct professional interviews and am comfortable assessing a candidate's qualifications and making recommendations to management. I am bilingual and am fluent in English and Spanish, both written and verbal.

The questions that follow the opening exchange varies and can address any topic relevant to the job, your experience or anything else. There is a list of some sample questions to anticipate at the end of this section. However, any question you may be asked is characterized as fitting into two distinct groups:

- **Informational**

- **Behavioral**

# Informational Questions

Informational questions are specific and are there to help the interviewer discover specific information about your qualifications for the position. They can be either Closed-Ended (yes or no, black or white, this or that) or Open-Ended, requiring a longer, more detailed and fact-filled response. Most of these questions will relate to your background, skills, education, experiences and other aspects of your work-related qualities. These should be relatively easy to respond to since they are factual and related to your specific circumstances. Answer these questions truthfully, thoughtfully and succinctly. The interviewer will ask follow-up questions or probe further if they want to learn more about a specific topic.

# Behavioral Questions

Behavioral questions are more complex and determine how you will respond to a specific situation or how you handled a similar challenge in the past. The interviewer will create a scenario related to something you may encounter in the position and will ask you to describe a solution to the issue. You should base your response either on a situation you have already dealt with in a previous position, or how you would use your experience and skills to address the situation.

The best way to respond to a behavioral question is to use a STAR strategy:

- Situation – Detail the background. Provide context (what, where when) a similar issue occurred during your previous employment.
- Task – Challenge, and expectations. What needed to be addressed? How did you determine this?
- Action – The action you took and why you choose this tactic.
- Result – What were the results? What would you do differently?

# Best/Worst Questions

Many interviewers will use a common strategy of asking you to describe your "Best" and "Worst" characteristics. The purpose of these questions is to determine your self-awareness and have you described the qualities you are most proud of. They are also trying to uncover hidden qualities that job candidates typically avoid and certainly do not list in their resumes. Most interviewers do not handle these questions well, but you still need to prepare yourself to respond to them.

The optimal way to respond to a request to describe your best characteristics is to list three to four qualities that will contribute to the company's business objectives. Your response should only include items which are directly related to the job you are interviewing for and should not address things like athleticism, attractiveness to the opposite gender or other personal traits not job-related.

When listing your worst qualities, you should take the opposite tack. Respond with characteristics that are not job-related. You can also list a quality that was previously an issue, but which you have resolved or are working to resolve. Examples of this may include: impatience, spending too much time addressing minor details of an issue or not being tolerant of people who don't do their share of the work.

## The Last Question

Invariably the interviewer will conclude the question and answer portion of the interview by asking you if you have any questions for them. Most job candidates will respond with a "No" or worse yet, will ask the wrong questions. This is a great opportunity for you to make an impression on the interviewer by responding affirmatively and by asking well thought out and interesting questions.

One of the reasons you need to perform research prior to the interview is to prepare for this question and the opportunity to ask the interviewer questions that you have prepared in advance. You should prepare three or more questions in each area that you researched: The Company, the Job, and the Interviewer. These should be clarifying questions; questions which elicit more details about the status of the company or the expectations for the job. You can refer to an item you discovered during your research, such as a recent change in the company's market performance or a new competitive threat and then ask what impact the interviewer expects this to have on the company or the job. You can ask how the job became available and whether the last person holding the position advanced within the company. You may refer to the fact that the interviewer has been with the company for many years and came there from one of the company's competitors. A good question to ask is, "why did you make the move and what has kept you with the organization for so long?

Questions like the ones described above will demonstrate several things to the hiring manager. They will confirm your interest in the position, demonstrate your efforts to prepare for the interview and reveal to them your knowledge of the organization's operations, market, competition and other business factors. These qualities will differentiate you from other candidates who are not as well prepared.

## Questions to Avoid

When asked if you have any questions for the interviewer, you should avoid any questions about compensation, benefits, time off, the opportunity for promotion or anything else not directly related to the duties and responsibilities of the job. It is not appropriate to ask these questions at this point of the interview process.

The best time to ask questions about compensation and benefits is when they offer you the position. This is one of the times when you have the most leverage in the hiring process and when you can get the best results. The company has indicated that they have selected you from amongst all the candidates they interviewed and should be willing to make concessions in these areas to ensure you accept the position. The next section on Negotiating the Job Offer will discuss this in further detail.

The night before the interview, review the questions that may come up and prepare a sound and brief responses. Ask a friend to help you rehearse some basic questions. Practice in front of a mirror until your presentation is natural and confident. Refer to the list of sample questions for additional help. You can find additional common interview questions on the Internet.

# Important Things You Need to Do

## During the Interview

- Research indicates most hiring decisions are made in the first five minutes of the interview. Yes, five minutes. Take a deep breath, be energized, be someone the interviewer will want to work with. (See "First Impressions" below.)
- Dress appropriately. Impressions matter. If you are not sure how formal to dress, phone the interviewer's assistant to ask what the typical work attire is. Dress at least this well or slightly better.
- Arrive early to your interview. Navigate to the appointment location beforehand so you are familiar with the commute.
- Assume that you will meet with the HR department, a direct manager and their manager, and possibly a person who manages a department you will be supporting in this new role.
- Make eye contact, shake hands firmly, and say it is a pleasure to meet them.
- Offer them your business card*
- Stay engaged during the interview. Observe the interviewer's body language for cues for moving from one subject to another.
- Remember that an interview is a two-way conversation. This is the time for you to ask questions you have about the position and company. If you sound insincere or bored, you will not get the job. Based on your pre-interview research, you should have at least nine prepared questions: three about the company, three about the position, and three about the interviewer.

- Stay calm and composed in the interview. Taking notes or bringing notes with you may help you relax through the conversation.
- LISTEN! Most people are so anxious about presenting themselves to the interviewer, they focus on what they are going to say rather than the information the interviewer is providing them. Even when they do listen, they listen to respond rather than to understand. When the interviewer is speaking, listen to what they are saying and try to focus on the information they are giving you. It can be helpful for the rest of the interview. Then, pause for two seconds before you respond. It signals to the interviewer that you were listening and gives you some time to prepare your response, based on their statements and what you learned from them.
- Learn from each interview. Use the experience as an opportunity to practice your interviewing skills and become more familiar with how interviews feel. Identify what you can do better next time and practice this before your next interview.

## At the End of the Interview

- Reiterate your interest in the job.
- Thank the interviewer or interviewers for their time.
- If you have not already, ask for the person's business card and give them yours.*
- Make eye contact, shake hands firmly, and say it was a pleasure to meet them.

*You can order cards from VistaPrint.com for less than $10

## Follow Up after the Interview

Send a thank you note to the interviewer the same day as the interview. Reiterate briefly why you are well qualified for the position and thank them for their time. An e-mail is generally appropriate, but sending a neatly hand-written note via regular mail is better. It is a nice way to remind the interviewer of who you are and why you are a good fit for the job. They will receive this in 1-2 days after the interview and it will remind them of you

## First Impressions

First impressions never count more than during a job interview. A recent CareerBuilder.com survey of over 2,700 hiring managers uncovered some common mistakes and a few humorous stories.

### Common Mistakes

- Inappropriate attire – 57%.
- Boredom or lack of interest – 55%.

- Criticizing a current or previous employer – 52%.
- Arrogant attitude – 51%.
- Answering a cell phone or texting during the interview – 46%.
- Vague answers – 34%.
- Not asking good questions – 34%.

**The Winners (Losers) in the "Hall of Shame"**

- One candidate wore a business suit and flip-flops.
- A job seeker asked if the interviewer wanted to meet later for a drink.
- An applicant for an accounting job said he was "bad at managing money."
- A candidate for a customer service job told the interviewer, "I don't really like working with people."
- A job seeker spent the entire interview staring at the ceiling.
- One person had to leave because his dog had gotten loose in the parking lot.

**Interviewers' Top 10 Pet Peeves with Interviewee (Who would do this?)**

1. Not knowing about the firm/company
2. Not asking any questions
3. Not bringing extra copy of your resume
4. Inappropriate attire
5. Bringing your Mom or Dad with you
6. Chewing gum
7. Not knowing what is on your resume
8. Asking when vacation pay starts
9. Taking a call during the interview
10. Being late

# Twenty Practice Interview Questions

---

*"Are you prepared with the answers? You need to be. Rehearse with a friend to be sure you are brief, coherent, and enthusiastic."* William Swansen

---

**1. Tell me about yourself.**

Talk only for 30-60 seconds. Do not talk about personal information in too much detail or in a negative light. Keep this part lighthearted and logical. Start anywhere; high school, college or your first job. Demonstrate your communication skills and linear thinking. Include some personal attributes that the employer will value.

**2. Why are you leaving your current position?**

This is a critical question. Do not "badmouth" a previous employer. Consider positive ways of explaining your separation. Relocation or a desire for advancement are both good responses.

**3. What do you consider your most significant accomplishment?**

This can get you the job. Prepare extensively (but be brief) with details and discuss personal involvement during a tough situation that required dedication to a specific goal.

**4. Why do you believe you are qualified for this position?**

Pick two or three main factors about the job and about you that are most relevant. Discuss specific details. Maybe select a technical skill, a specific management skill (organizing, staffing, planning), or a personal success.

**5. Have you ever accomplished something you didn't think you could?**

The Interviewer is trying to determine your goal orientation, work ethic, personal commitment, and integrity. Provide an example where you overcame numerous difficulties to succeed. Show you are not a quitter, and that you will get going when the going gets tough. This can be either career related or personal.

**6. What do you like or dislike most about your current position?**

The Interviewer is trying to determine compatibility with an open position. Stating your dislike of overtime or voicing vague opinions about "management" can cost you the job. There is nothing wrong with liking challenges, pressure situations, opportunities to grow, or disliking bureaucracy and frustrating situations. (But many jobs include some frustrations ....) Just be cautious in how you present this to the interviewer. You always want to sound positive and professional.

**7. How do you handle pressure? Do you like or dislike these situations?**

High achievers tend to perform well in high-pressure situations. There is nothing wrong with this if you know what you are going into. If you do perform well under stress, provide a good example with details, giving an overview of the stressful situation. If you do not handle stress or pressure well, be sure to touch on a strategy or two that you use to manage pressure and give at least one positive anecdote of successfully doing so.

**8. A valued employee shows initiative. Describe when you have shown initiative.**

A proactive, results-oriented person doesn't have to be told what to do. To convince the interviewer you possess this trait you must give a series of brief examples describing your self-motivation. Ask yourself when did you do something, without being asked, that benefited the company.

**9. Describe a difficult business situation. With hindsight, what would you have done differently?**

Employers use this question to learn how introspective you are and to see if you can learn from your mistakes. It indicates an open, more flexible personality. Don't be afraid to talk about your failures, but only if you have learned from them. This is a critical aspect of high potential individuals. Just be sure to stay positive when describing the tough situation.

**10. How have you grown or changed over the past few years?**

This requires thought. They are looking for answers such as:

- Growth in technical skills, or increased self-confidence, which are important aspects of personal development.
- Discussing this effectively is indicative of a well-balanced, intelligent person.
- Overcoming personal obstacles or weaknesses can brand you as an approachable and able employee.

## 11. What do you consider your most significant strengths?

Be prepared. Know your four or five key strengths. Be able to discuss each with a specific example. Select those attributes that are most compatible with the job opening.

## 12. What do you consider your most significant weaknesses?

Do not reveal deep character flaws. Rather discuss tolerable faults that you are working towards improving. Better still, show how a weakness can become a strength. For example, how concentration on details results in higher quality work even though it requires extra time.

## 13. Deadlines, frustrations, difficult people, and silly rules can make a job difficult. How do you handle these types of situations?

Most companies, unfortunately, face these problems daily. If you cannot deal with petty frustrations, you will be seen as a potential problem. You certainly can state your displeasure with inefficiency and pettiness, but how you overcome these issues is more important. Be sure to explain what you have learned along the way.

## 14. One of our biggest problems is_____. What has been your experience with it? How would you deal with it?

Think on your feet. Ask questions to get details. State how you would go about solving the problem. Be specific. Show your organizational and analytical skills. Keep it simple. You may want to say you would want to seek advice before acting.

## 15. How do you compare your technical skills to your management skills?

Many people tend to minimize their technical skills, either because they do not have any, or they don't like getting into details. Most successful employees possess good technical skills and get into enough detail to make sure they understand the information presented to them. Aim for a good balance to be seriously considered for the position.

## 16. How has your technical ability been important in accomplishing results?

Clearly, the interviewer believes he needs a strong level of technical competence. Most strong employees have good technical backgrounds, even if they have gone beyond just details. Describe specific examples of your technical wherewithal, but don't be afraid to say you are not current in some areas but appreciate the need to learn.

**17. How would you handle a situation with tight deadlines, low employee morale, and inadequate resources?**

If you pull this off effectively, it indicates you have strong management skills. You need to be creative; An example would be great. Relate your toughest management task, even if it doesn't meet all the criteria. Organizational skills, interpersonal skills, and handling pressure are key elements of effective management.

**18. Are you satisfied with your career to date? What would you change if you could?**

Be honest. Interviewers want to know if they can keep you happy. It is important to know if you are willing to make some sacrifices to get your career on the right track. Lack of motivation is an instant rejection. Perhaps you are not entirely satisfied. At least touch on a few areas of your career path that you are proud of. Mention how exciting the opportunity to even interview for a position with career growth is.

**19. What are your career goals? Where do you see yourself five years from now?**

Most importantly, be realistic! Pie-in-the-sky stuff brands you as immature. One or two promotions in three to five years is a reasonable goal. This is when you can mention one or two of your long-term career goals.

**20. Why hire you for this position? What kind of contribution would you make?**

This question offers you a good chance to summarize why they should hire you. By now you know their key problems. Restate them and show how you would address them. Relate to specific attributes and specific accomplishments. Qualify responses with the need to gather information. Don't be cocky. Demonstrate a thoughtful, organized, strong effort attitude. Always be honest. How would you help the company achieve both its short-term and long-term goals?

# Negotiating the Job Offer

---

*"To be a great champion, you must believe you are the best. If you're not, pretend you are." —Muhammad Ali*

---

Congratulations! They offered you the job. Now what? This can be the best but also the most challenging part of the job search process. After either a long period of unemployment or a grueling job search process, most people will quickly accept the job offer made by the employer. However, this can be a large mistake and have implications far beyond the initial job.

Once you have received a job offer, the power in the job search process has temporarily shifted in your favor. The employer has indicated that they would prefer to hire you rather than the other prospects they have interviewed and are anxious to bring you into the company. While this is great news, it also provides you the opportunity to negotiate not only the salary but other benefits and most importantly, your growth path within the company. It is important that you take a minute to pause and reflect on what you really want to get from this position. You only have one chance to do this correctly.

Many people will hesitate to negotiate a job offer, fearing that it may jeopardize their opportunity to join the company. Just the opposite is true. Negotiating the job offer will set a tone with your employer that while you respect them, they also need to respect you. It gives you the opportunity to maximize your compensation and possibly your benefits package. You can negotiate your growth path within the company to some degree by requesting specific reviews and opportunities for advancement.

## Salary

The easiest part of the job offer to negotiate is the compensation. It is very important not to address this prior to the job offer if possible. As a prospective employee, you should never raise this issue during the interview process. If the employer asks you about compensation prior to offering you the job, it is best to answer by providing them a range of salaries based on research you have done for the position you are seeking. The conversation will go something like this when the employer asks you what sort of compensation you are looking for:

"I have researched the compensation for this position and the average for your industry ranges from a low of $40,000 to $60,000 at the high end. Naturally, research bases these numbers on an individual's skills and experience. I believe I fall in the middle of this range."

You can also state that based on your qualifications you are at the lower or higher end of the range. This allows you to answer the question without locking into a specific salary or being disqualified because of your compensation requirements. NOTE: it is important that you have done prior research on the compensation range for the position you are seeking. You have to be confident about the range you are providing the employer and base it on data you can cite if asked to.

Once you have received a job offer everything changes. You now have the leverage to seek a salary which you think is fair to both you and the employer. The negotiation can go two different ways. The first begins with the employer offering you a specific compensation package. The second is they ask you what sort of compensation you require. In either case, you use the same strategy as detailed above. State that you have done some research and that you have found that the range for the position you are being offered is between a minimum and maximum. Based on your qualifications, you feel that you fall at a specific point within the range.

The employer may agree with this, or they will stick to their original offer. They may justify the offer based on their budget or the current compensation plans for other people within the company. If you get the feeling that they will not budge off of this number and you would like to accept it to get the position, then you still have one more task. When you accept that compensation package, let them know that you would like to schedule a performance review at a specific date or period in the future. At that time, you would like to the opportunity to discuss an increase in salary based on your performance and/or meeting the expectations of the employer.

Salary negotiation is an inexact science at best. You must do your best, based on your personal style and your feelings about the flexibility the employer has in offering you a compensation package. Accepting the original compensation is OK If you think it is fair and it meets your requirements. However, never hesitate to try to negotiate. You will never get what you don't ask for, and you will never have the same leverage you have when they have just offered you the position.

# Benefits

Benefits such as vacation time, health coverage, 401K programs and other items typically offered by employers are more difficult to negotiate. These are usually standard company-wide and based on either the length of employment or the level of seniority within the organization.

Before trying to negotiate the benefits package, read it thoroughly and make sure you understand it. If you feel there are some options to improve the benefits package, by all means, attempt to negotiate these. Options may include additional personal time off, flexible work schedules, the opportunity to work at home or other non-financial aspects of the benefits package.

Insurance coverage is typically standard across the company and non-negotiable. The same is true for retirement plans including pensions and 401K programs.

# Job Advancement

Job Advancement is the last item of the job offer that is negotiable. This is the opportunity to advance within the new organization, either through promotions or internal transfers. These types of advancements are typically based on tenure with the company, performance in the position, job reviews and ratings, additional training, and experience obtained on the job.

Again, the best time to negotiate for future job advancement is once you have received an offer and prior to accepting the position. While you cannot outright ask for specific job advancement opportunities at specific times, you can ensure that the company offers you opportunities for advancement when it is appropriate. This is not a formal negotiation, but more of a discussion with your hiring manager. It is OK to ask them about future advancement opportunities and what the job you are being offered may lead to. Once they describe some of these, the next thing to talk about is what you will need to do in order to position yourself for advancement into these positions. Make sure you take some notes during the conversation which you can refer back to in the future.

You should also ask about performance reviews and when they will occur. If the company doesn't have a formal review process, then request that your manager offer you the opportunity for review after a reasonable period of time. This will be important in positioning you for future advancement and to ensure that you are meeting the expectations for the position during the early stages of your employment. More about this later.

## Conclusion

Whether you are a skilled negotiator, extremely confident or terribly shy, the best time to negotiate for anything related to a job is after you have received an offer and before you accept the position. Jeopardizing the job offer is possible, based on how aggressively you negotiate, and the items you negotiate for. The key is to have a strategy prior to receiving the job offer and knowing what you need and what you are willing to compromise on to get the job. There is no perfect negotiation, except the one that you execute.

# The First 90 Days; The Key to Success and Advancement

---

*"If one advances confidently in the direction of his dreams, and endeavors to live the life which he has imagined, he will meet with a success unexpected in common hours." —Henry David Thoreau*

---

T he first 90 days of a new job are the most critical. They can either ensure your future success with the organization or make it more difficult to integrate yourself into your new position. Here are some tips to help you started on the right foot and be successful.

## Understand Your Job

During the first week, meet with your supervisor to discuss what your specific job description is and the duties associated with it. Topics of the discussion can include:

- Specific Title and Job Description
- Duties of the Position
- Start-Up Plan: What to expect during the first 2-4 Weeks
  1. Orientation
  2. Training
  3. Feedback
  4. Next Steps
- What will you be doing? Specific daily, weekly and monthly activities
- Who will you be reporting to and accountable to (this may be one or several people)
- Deliverables: What are you expected to produce, deliver, or contribute? (Be very specific on this topic)
- Metrics: How they will measure your activities and evaluate you

- Development Plan; What will be the plan to increase your skills and abilities after you have become proficient at the current position

## Select a Mentor

Find the right person-

- Someone who has longevity with the organization
- Someone you are comfortable talking to
- Someone near your age (not critical, but this may be easier)
- Someone who has experience in your position/department/job description, etc...

The purpose of this is to have someone you can...

- Ask advice of
- Ask the "dumb questions" you may feel uncomfortable asking your supervisor
- Solicit feedback from
- Get referrals to other people in the company who you either need to interact with or would like to get to know

## Solicit Feedback

Ask your supervisor for a quick (5-10 minute) meeting to discuss how you are doing and what you could do differently. (You should do this every two weeks during the first month then every 4 weeks during month 2 and 3 of the first 90 days.)

Conduct Informal 360 Degree Reviews; Quick, informal feedback from your peers and people you interact with. A simple question may be, "What is the one thing I could do differently to improve how we work together?"

## Network

- Identify people within the organization that you would like to get to know better and who can help you advance within the organization or provide you other opportunities.
- Get to know them through an introduction from your supervisor, mentor or co-workers.
- Be genuine; make sure you are really interested in them as an individual and not just for what they can help you with.
- "Give to Get." Offer something of interest to them. It will probably be something from outside of the company since you are the "New Kid on the Block." It could be:
  - An introduction to someone from your former companies or any of your acquaintances.

- o  A recommendation of a good book or another resource to help them in their job.
- o  Information specific to one of their interests.
- Maintain the relationship. This is not an event but rather a process. Touch base frequently with your network and continue to provide them value on a regular basis.

By following these guidelines during the first 90 Days on a new job, you are more likely to be successful, advance within the company, and earn more money. Most importantly it will prepare you for the next step in your career path. You are also more likely to be happy in the new position, which will contribute to your success and advancement.

# Job Search Techniques – Using a Systematic Approach to Find a Job

J

ob hunting is a challenging task even in the best of times. It becomes even more challenging when the economy is in a slump or there are fewer jobs available, with more people competing for them. This requires the job hunter to become more creative and use all the tools and resources available to them to be more efficient and effective.

## Become a Sales Person

One way to increase your chances of finding a position is to take a systematic approach to looking for a job. What exactly does a system mean? In this case, it is using the same techniques that professional salespeople use to sell their products. If you think about it, you provide a service and the result of your job search activities should be getting a contract with an employer who is willing to compensate you for your services. If you accept this premise, implementing a systematic process to accomplish this will make it very easy. You should consider using a step-by-step process which will enable you to get a job in about 45 - 90 days. The secret is to commit to this and to adhere to the plan which incorporates a rigid schedule, specific activities and a commitment to follow through. These are the same components critical to success with any other important objective you are attempting to achieve.

When you are looking for a job, you should do what salespeople do every day when they are selling their company's products and services.

- Send out a lot of information such as product literature, specification sheets, and informational flyers to try to get a prospect's attention. In your case, these are resumes, cover letters, and an up to date LinkedIn profile.
- Follow up with phone calls, notes, emails and other forms of communication to start a dialog with your prospective customers (employers.)
- Make them aware of the need for your services (talents, skills, and experiences.)
- Differentiate yourself from your competitors.
- Convince them that your sales claims are true (you have the ability to do the job.)
- It is a numbers game: 100 letters and phone calls will get you 10 conversations, which will get you 3 interviews, which may lead one job offer.
- Success comes from 3 things: Hard Work, Timing, and Luck, with Hard Work being the most important.

## Go to Work

Since you are trying to sell something, you need to go to "work." Your new job is finding a job. If you do the work and follow the plan outlined below, you will close the sale (i.e., find a job.)

The general plan is:

Commit to "working" 8 hours a day. This consists of:

- Working at a temporary job to pay your living expenses.
- Volunteering or doing some other activity which helps you get to know a profession, industry or specific employer of interest to you.
- Using the "Selling Yourself Into a Job" system to find permanent employment.

The objective is to put in a 40-hour week which includes all three of these activities.

Your day starts at 8:00 a.m. and ends at 5:00 p.m., 5 days a week unless the temporary job or volunteer position requires time during evenings or on weekends. You should try to maximize the time you spend at the temporary job and volunteering. One gives you money and the other provides you with experience and exposure to potential employers.

When you are not working or volunteering, you need to be doing the same things a salesperson does every day:

- Researching potential employers
- Visiting Job Search websites looking for tips and tricks. Become a professional job seeker by educating yourself, just like you would for any other profession

- Improving your resume, cover letter, and LinkedIn profile. This may include customizing it for a specific job opportunity
- Sending out emails with your resume to target hiring managers
- Applying on company websites (although you shouldn't spend too much time doing this)
- Making follow-up calls
- Going to interviews

## Get Some Help

Here is where you may need additional help:

- Finding information on companies and the contacts at the companies you want to apply to, using tools like LinkedIn, Data.com, etc.
- Reviewing and editing your resume, cover letters, and LinkedIn profile
- Getting guidance on interview techniques and business conversations
- Keeping on track with your activities, focus, and results
- Finding tips to help you manage your time and be more effective (i.e., blind copying yourself on every email you send out, so you can reuse it and not have to create everything from scratch)
- Preparing interview plans and strategies (company research, timing the commute, a list of questions for the interview, etc.)
- Debriefing after each interview to see how you can improve on them

The resources you need to assist with these items are readily available from a variety of sources. These include job boards (Indeed, Glassdoor, Monster, etc.,) career coaches, temp agencies, state and local unemployment agencies, and independent job resources.

## The Plan

The plan you develop must have a specific goal, a set of objectives and an activity schedule. The goal is to find a job in 45- 90 days (accept the fact that it might take this long.) The objective is to get at least one interview a week after the first 3 weeks. The daily activity schedule may look like this:

- Research and collect information on 10 target employers
- Send out 10 resumes to the prospective employers
- Apply online to 10 prospective employers
- Send out 10 follow up emails to jobs you have already applied to
- Make 10 follow up calls

Don't worry if this sounds overwhelming. Once you begin working on this and have the research tools, a library of resumes and cover letters and a workflow setup, this will become easy. This methodology is classic Sales 101. It may take some time, but it will eventually be successful.

## The Schedule

During that first week, all you need to do is to locate 10 target employers per day. You will need to determine who you should be communicating with and identify their contact information. You will also need to do some research on their website to learn more about the company. Begin to craft a reason why you would like to work with them for the email you will be sending them. By the end of the week, you will have a list of 50 target employers.

Here is the schedule for the next and subsequent weeks:

- **Monday** – Begin to send out 10 resumes and apply online to 10 companies. You also need to research another 10 companies and add them to your list.

- **Tuesday** – Send out 10 resumes and apply to 10 companies online each day. Research another 10 companies and add them to your list.

- **Wednesday** – Send out 10 resumes and apply to 10 companies online each day. Research another 10 companies and add them to your list. Begin to send out follow up emails to the companies that you applied to two days earlier (Monday.)

- **Thursday** – Send out 10 resumes and apply to 10 companies online each day. Research another 10 companies and add them to your list. Send out follow up emails to the companies that you applied to two days earlier (Tuesday.)

- **Friday** – Send out 10 resumes and apply to 10 companies online each day. Research another 10 companies and add them to your list. Send out follow up emails to the companies that you applied to two days earlier. Begin to call the companies you sent the follow-up emails to two days earlier (Wednesday.) You should have a series of telephone scripts for this activity, so you will know what you are going to say when you get somebody on the phone.

Repeat the activities you did on the previous Friday daily.

Initially, there may be little or no response from the companies you have contacted. However, during the third week, you should start hearing back from the employers. Often it will be a polite email, call, or letter explaining that there currently were no positions available, but they will keep your information on file. Sometimes the employer will ask for additional information about your background, skills or experience. On a couple of occasions, they may have you come in for a group interview, at which there may be as many as 30 applicants in attendance. Don't let this discourage you. It is a part of the process.

Soon you will begin getting invitations for interviews. This should be encouraging, even though several of the opportunities may be for positions you are not interested in for a variety of reasons, including location, the industry, company or specific position. However, you should go on every interview to either genuinely apply for the position or to practice and refine your interview skills.

By the fifth week, it should become apparent that the program is beginning to pay off. By this time, you will have contacted over 150 companies, followed up with most of them, and will begin getting callbacks and interview requests on a regular basis. By putting enough information about yourself out into the job market, people will begin to respond.

## Why It Works

You will be successful in reaching your goal of finding a job using the "Selling Yourself Into a Job" system for the following reasons:

- The structure of the process provides a framework to execute the job search in a regular and systematic way.

- There are specific goals, objectives, and processes which drive the process and will keep you focused.

- Every day will require specific activities, and these will keep you accountable.

- A structured, repeatable process makes the tasks easier the more you do them. This reduces the time required to do the tasks which should encourage you to continue to complete them.

- Getting results in only a few weeks will motivate you to continue to execute the plan.

- You will become more comfortable and confident when you do things that you have done before and are familiar with. There will be a noticeable change in your communication skills and confidence level several weeks into the process.

- The resources used during the process will help keep you focused and will provide good advice and tips on creating resumes, writing cover letters, developing phone scripts and improving your interview behaviors.

This process can work for anybody. The key elements are:

- Treat the process like a job. Your job is to find a job.

- There is a definitive schedule. You wake up every morning knowing exactly what you need be doing in terms of your job search process.

- Locating additional resources which will help you in this process. Websites, online resources, tips, and tricks related to your job search.

- The more you do the process, the more repetitive it is, the easier it is going to be, and the better you are going to become at it.

# Conclusion

---

*"No one ever gets very far unless he accomplishes the impossible at least once a day."* —Elbert Hubbard

---

A s stated in the forward of this book, the goal was to make the job search process easier and to provide you with a set of guidelines you can follow to execute each component of your job search. You start by evaluating your career goals and creating a plan for your career advancement. This includes your ultimate goal and your first step. What comes between these depends on how well you execute your job search and perform the jobs you do as you progress toward your final position.

After you have developed a plan, you need to create your "Job Search Collateral" materials. These are your resume, cover letter, and LinkedIn profile. As you compose these, keep in mind that you are writing for the audience, i.e., the employer. Don't fall into the trap of creating a glowing description of your professional experience and skill sets. While these are important, present these in a clear, concise and compelling manner. If they don't address the needs of the employer, then you have missed the mark.

The next step is to identify prospective employers. You do this by reviewing the criteria that are important to you and then utilizing the resources available online and within your network of friends and business associates. Keep in mind that 80% of people are hired due to a referral, so networking is the key to finding a job.

Once you have begun sending out cover letters and resumes to prospective employers and leveraging your network, you will begin to receive interview invitations. Keep in mind that the most important part of the interview occurs before you arrive. This is the preparation you do to get ready for the interview. It starts with researching the company, the position and the people you will be interviewing with. You also need to anticipate the questions which will be asked and practice your responses. There are many resources available to help you with this both online and among your friends and associates. The better prepared you are for the interview, the better you will do. Also, keep in mind that the interview is not over until you have followed up by sending a thank you email and note to the employer, emphasizing your enthusiasm for the position and reflecting on some of the key points of the interview.

The job search process does not stop once you receive an offer for the position. This is one of the most critical steps in the process because it can determine both your compensation and career advancement opportunities once you accept the job. It is one of the few times that you have the most leverage and you need to take advantage of it. You have to get out of your comfort zone and be willing to make a few demands on the employer. It is unlikely that you will jeopardize your chance of getting the job by doing this and the upside is worth the small risk.

The last part of the job search process actually occurs once you begin working in the position. There are specific things you can do during the first 90 days on the job to ensure your success in the position and future advancement either with the organization you are working for or during subsequent jobs. Make sure you understand the job duties and your employer's expectations for you. Find a mentor who can coach you and help you integrate into the organization. Solicit feedback from your supervisor and the people you interact with on the job. Getting feedback early allows you to correct anything that you may be doing incorrectly. Finally, continue to network both within your organization and among your other business associates. The best time to begin to look for your next job is immediately after you started your current one.

Hopefully, you have found this book helpful and have executed some of the strategies and actions recommended for one or more elements of your job search. If so, then it is very likely that you are well on your way to your next job and eventually to your "Dream Job." As stated at the beginning of the book, "Once you find your dream job, you will never work a day in your life!"

Good luck with your job search and best wishes for a successful career, and the benefits it brings to the rest of your life.

www.ingramcontent.com/pod-product-compliance
Lightning Source LLC
Chambersburg PA
CBHW052333220526
45472CB00001B/402